SERIES EDITOR: JOHN MOOR

ORDER OF BATTLE SERIES:

GETTYSBURG

CONFEDERATE:
THE ARMY OF NORTHERN VIRGINIA
1 JULY 1863

JAMES ARNOLD & ROBERTA WIENER

First published in Great Britain in 1998 by Osprey Publishing, Elms Court, Chapel Way, Botley, Oxford OX2 9LP United Kingdom

ISBN 1 85532 834 8

Osprey Series Editor: Lee Johnson
Ravelin Series Editor: John Moore
Research Co-ordinator: Diane Moore
Design: Ravelin Limited, Braceborough, Lincolnshire, United Kingdom
Origination by Valhaven Ltd, Isleworth, United Kingdom
Printed through Worldprint Ltd, Hong Kong

98 99 00 01 02   10 9 8 7 6 5 4 3 2 1

FOR A CATALOGUE OF ALL BOOKS PUBLISHED BY OSPERY MILITARY, AUTOMOTIVE AND AVIATION PLEASE WRITE TO:
The Marketing Manager, Osprey Publishing Ltd., P.O. Box 140, Wellingborough, Northants, NN8 4ZA United Kingdom

Key to Military Series symbols

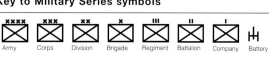

Series style

The style of presentation adopted in the Order of Battle series is designed to provide quickly the maximum information for the reader.

Order of Battle Unit Diagrams – All 'active' units in the ORBAT, that is those present and engaged on the battlefield are drawn in black. Those units not yet arrived or those present on the battlefield but unengaged are 'shadowed'.

Unit Data Panels – Similarly, those units which are present and engaged are provided with company details for infantry and cavalry bodies and with details of the pieces for artillery.

Battlefield Maps – Units engaged are shown in the respective colours of their armies. Units shown as 'shadowed' are those deployed for battle but not engaged at the time.

Order of Battle Timelines

Battle Page Timelines – Each volume concerns the Order of Battle for the armies involved. Rarely are the forces available to a commander committed into action as per his ORBAT. To help the reader follow the sequence of events, a Timeline is provided at the bottom of each 'battle' page. This Timeline gives the following information:

The top line bar defines the actual time of the actions being described in that battle section.

The middle line shows the time period covered by the whole day's action.

The bottom line indicates the page numbers of the other, often interlinked, actions covered in this book.

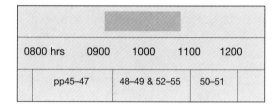

Publisher's note

Readers may wish to study this title in conjunction with the following Osprey publications:

MAA 170 *American Civil War Armies (1) Confederate*
MAA 177 *American Civil War Armies (2) Union*
MAA 179 *American Civil War Armies (3) Specialist Troops*
MAA 190 *American Civil War Armies (4) State Troops*
MAA 207 *American Civil War Armies (5) Volunteer Militias*
CAM 10 *First Bull Run 1861*
CAM 17 *Chickamauga 1863*
CAM 26 *Vicksburg 1863*
CAM 32 *Antietam 1862*
CAM 52 *Gettysburg 1863*
CAM 54 *Shiloh 1862*
CAM 55 *Chancellorsville 1863*

Editor's note

Wherever possible primary sources have been used in compiling the information in this volume.

CONTENTS

THE ARMY OF NORTHERN VIRGINIA

Lee Marches North

On June 25, 1863, while en route to Gettysburg, Robert E. Lee wrote to President Jefferson Davis to describe the strategic concept undergirding his invasion of the North: "It seems to me that we cannot afford to keep our troops awaiting possible movements of the enemy, but that our true policy is...to employ our own forces as to give occupation to his at points of our selection." With this statement Lee was articulating an offensive grand strategy. He continued, "our concentration at any point compels that of the enemy." Lee recognised that his march north would compel the Federal army to follow. A confrontation was certain to ensue. Given Lee's preference for the tactical offensive, it was likely to feature a Confederate attack.

The origins of the campaign grew out of the army's great victory at Chancellorsville back in May. Although it was already being hailed as 'Lee's masterpiece', Lee himself was dissatisfied with its results. By his assessment, the army had had an opportunity to destroy Hooker's Army of the Potomac and had failed. Hooker had managed to extricate his army and retreat to safety behind the Rappahannock River. It reminded Lee of his victory at Second Manassas, another incomplete success due to the ability of the Federal army to retire into the impregnable Washington, D.C. defences.

As he pondered what to do after Chancellorsville, Lee ached for a battlefield from which the Union army could not escape by retiring behind either a natural or man-made defence. Furthermore, the army had won at Chancellorsville without the presence of half of James Longstreet's I Corps. What it might accomplish when fully concentrated excited the army commander.

In mid-May Lee travelled to Richmond to meet with Davis. For the past week he had been exchanging messages with the War Department regarding the possibility of sending men west to help defend Vicksburg. Lee firmly opposed the idea, saying "it becomes a question between Virginia and the Mississippi." He acknowledged that something drastic had to be done

General Robert Edward Lee. He arrived on the battlefield some six hours after Heth's Division first deployed against the Union troops west of Gettysburg.

and proposed a second invasion of the North. It might or might not relieve the pressure in the west, but in the past Lincoln had shown a special sensitivity to threats to his capital by summoning troops to its defence. Moreover, there was the chance that a victory gained north of the Potomac would actually lead to

THE ARMY OF NORTHERN VIRGINIA - GETTYSBURG - July 1

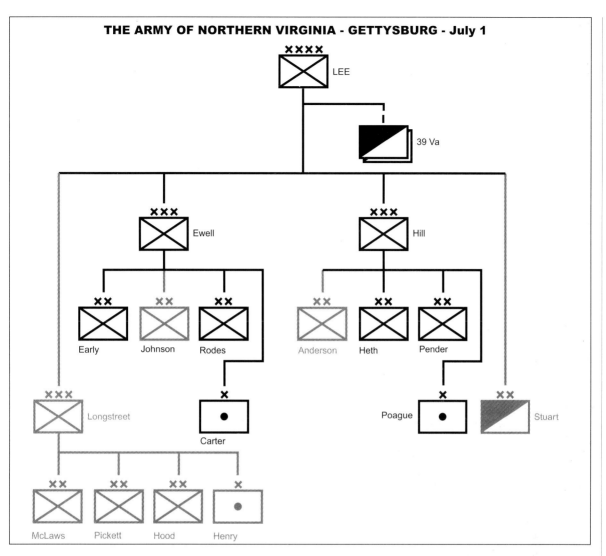

Washington's capture and foreign intervention on behalf of the Confederacy. Davis and his Cabinet reflected upon all of this and upon the fact that since Lee had taken command of the Army of Northern Virginia he had never lost a battle. The Davis government authorised Lee to march north.

When Stonewall Jackson died, Lee said, "I do not know how to replace him." Rather than try, he decided

---

17 Staff and Field Officers

Escort/Couriers
39th Battalion Virginia Cavalry
Major John Harvie Richardson
60 troops present for duty equipped

Co. A Captain Augustus Pifer's Co.
Co. C Lee's Body Guard Co. B

Gettysburg was a classic 'encounter' battle. On the first day, neither Lee nor Meade had all their forces available for action. From the evening of July 1, as fresh divisions and brigades reached the battlefield, the options widened for both commanders, but less so for Lee. On the first day the absence of Stuart's cavalry, though only 23 miles away, prevented the Confederate forces from exploiting the Federal reverse after they were driven out of Gettysburg.

to abandon the army's two corps structure and create a triangular structure of three infantry corps with three divisions each. He believed that "our army would be invincible if it could be properly organised and officered."

Lee retained the dependable Longstreet as commander of I Corps. He chose Richard Ewell to lead II Corps. Ewell had served only briefly under Lee, but he

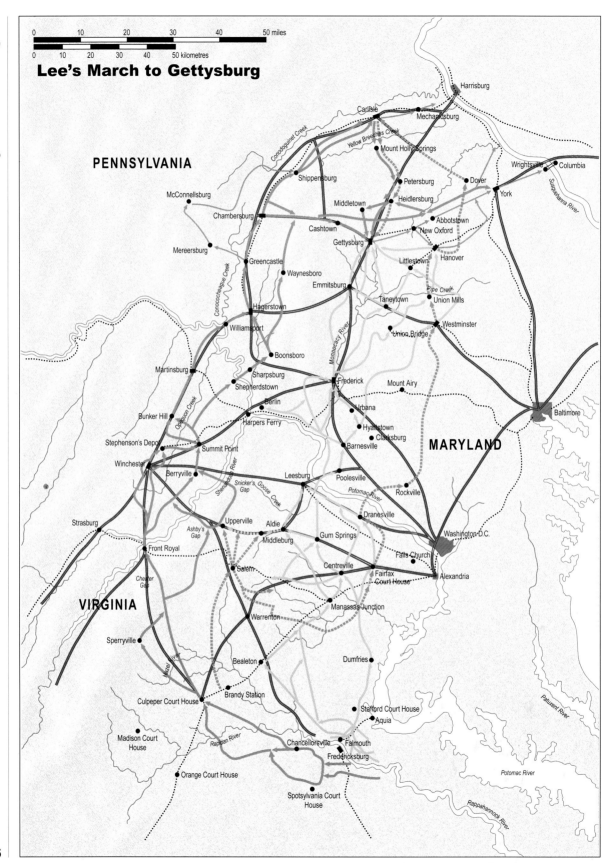

Lee's March to Gettysburg

Brigadier-General William Nelson Pendleton, a West Point graduate, was aged 53, sickly and unsuited for command and yet remained a Lee favourite.

knew that II Corps' soldiers liked and respected him. He considered Ewell "an honest, brave soldier, who has always done his duty well." He worried that Ewell was accustomed to close supervision and would now have to exercise independent judgement. In contrast to his tepid praise for Ewell was his attitude toward his choice to command III Corps, A.P. Hill.

In October 1862, Lee had described A.P. Hill as his best divisional commander and a man who "fights his troops well and takes good care of them." Hill marched to Gettysburg possessing Lee's full confidence.

The army had lost more than eighteen percent of its strength at Chancellorsville. It had been particularly hard hit by casualties among its mid-level command. Not only would two of the army's three infantry corps be under recently elevated officers, five of nine divisions were led by men who previously had served

CSA Organisation at Gettysburg

CAVALRY

DIVISION
(6,400 men)
6 Brigades
+ 1 Horse Artillery Battalion
+ 1 Independent Command
BRIGADE
(900-1,900 men)
2-6 Cavalry Regiments/Battalions
REGIMENT
(145-1,090 men)
Normally 10 Companies/Troops
BATTALION
(125-170 men)
Normally 5-7 Companies
COMPANY/TROOP
(60 men)

either briefly or not at all in their present capacities. The army's brigadiers were its acknowledged backbone. But six brigades were under new command and six more were commanded by colonels whom Lee judged unready for promotion.

These deficiencies would become apparent at the battle. But on the eve of the campaign Lee put his faith in his vaunted rank and file. He said, "They will go anywhere and do anything if properly led."

Lee also redistributed his artillery. He abolished the general reserve and assigned five artillery battalions to each of the three corps. Brigadier-General William Pendleton retained his post as Chief of Artillery, but it now became a nominal assignment.

Stuart's Cavalry gained three brigades of Virginia cavalry in order to reinforce his existing three.

Overall, the accretion of force, supplemented by volunteers and conscripts, brought the Army of Virginia almost up to the strength it had enjoyed before the Fredericksburg and Chancellorsville campaigns.

In early June Lee began shifting his army secretly westward for a march up the Shenandoah and Cumberland Valleys. By holding the passes in the Blue Ridge and South Mountains, he could screen his advance and protect his supply line.

By June 17 the army was strung out over a 100-mile distance. By June 24 it had closed up north of the Potomac. After that it enjoyed easy, uneventful marches until the encounter at Gettysburg.

CSA Organisation at Gettysburg

INFANTRY

CORPS
(20,800-26,700 men)
3 Infantry Divisions
+ Corps Reserve Artillery
DIVISION
(5,400-7,300 men)
3-4 Infantry Brigades
+ Divisional Artillery Brigade
BRIGADE
(740-2,580 men)
3-6 Infantry Regiments/Battalions
REGIMENT
(135-840 men)
Normally 10 Companies
BATTALION
(130-400 men)
Normally 4-7 Companies
COMPANY
(35-40 men)

THE ARMY OF NORTHERN VIRGINIA

I CSA Army Corps

I Corps came into existence when Lee reorganised the army in 1862 after the Seven Days' Battles. While Jackson's II Corps manoeuvred brilliantly to set up the opponent during the Second Manassas Campaign, it was I Corps that provided the powerful knockout punch.

Lieutenant-General James Longstreet, an undistinguished student at West Point and a former U.S. Army paymaster, at age 43 proved a skilled and fearless battlefield commander for the Confederates.

At the Battle of Sharpsburg, I Corps fought a bloody defensive battle. On this field, Lee greeted its commander, James P. Longstreet, with a rare departure from his usual reserve, embracing him with the words "Here's my old war-horse at last." By occupying good defensive ground at Fredericksburg, the Corps conserved Confederate lives and helped repel Union assaults. For Longstreet, promoted to lieutenant-general in October 1862, Fredericksburg was a tactical model showing how the Corps would compete with the numerically superior Federal army.

Half of the Corps was on detached service around Suffolk, Virginia during the Chancellorsville Campaign.

16 Staff and Field Officers

McLaws' and Anderson's Divisions remained with Lee's army.

In the reorganisation following Jackson's death, the Corps shed Anderson's division but, unlike the other two infantry corps, otherwise remained intact. The Corps' divisional command structure also enjoyed a constancy unlike its sister corps. The same divisional leaders - McLaws, Hood, and Pickett - commanded the same basic forces at Fredericksburg and at Gettysburg.

Officers and men trusted Longstreet. They understood that while he was personally fearless on the battlefield, he believed victory came from thorough planning rather than reckless heroism. Longstreet, in turn, was undoubtedly the most seasoned and reliable of Lee's remaining lieutenants. While he supported Lee's bold strategic offensives, he wanted to manoeuvre to obtain a favourable defensive position that would compel a Union attack. In this predilection lay the seeds for mis-understanding and disaster.

June 30 found Hood and McLaws at Greenwood, about 14 miles from Gettysburg, and Pickett guarding the rear at Chambersburg another 11 miles distant.

I CORPS
(not arrived at Gettysburg by the end of fighting on July 1)
Lieutenant-General James Longstreet

McLaws' Division
Major-General Lafayette McLaws
Pickett's Division
Major-General George Edward Pickett
Hood's Division
Major-General John Bell Hood
I Corps Reserve Artillery
Colonel James Burdge Walton

I CSA Corps Casualties at Gettysburg
1st July 1863

Corps not engaged

8

I CSA ARMY CORPS - GETTYSBURG - July 1

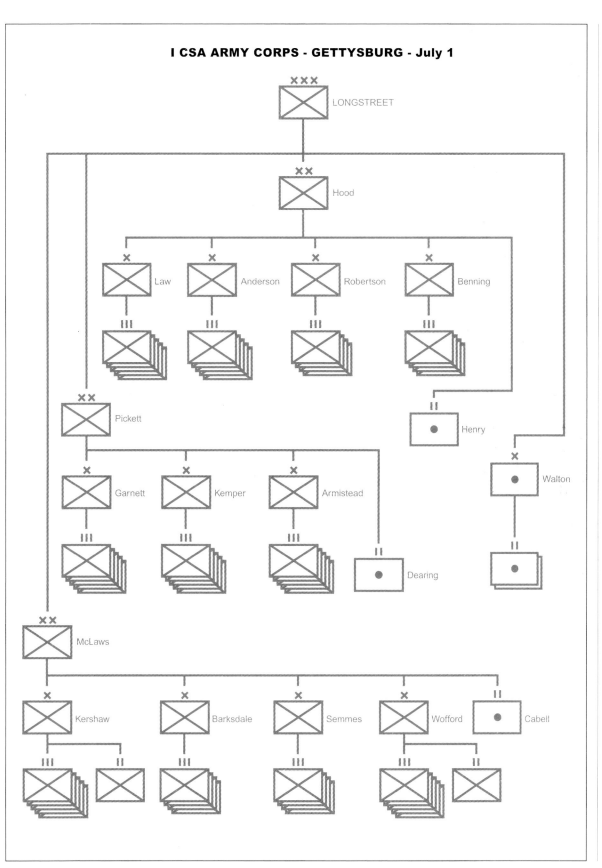

I CSA Army Corps - McLaws' Division

General Lafayette McLaws and his Division began their association in November 1861. The Division manned the Yorktown defences and was present when McClellan's Army of the Potomac arrived the next spring. Although McLaws himself was a West Point graduate and had served with the infantry in Mexico, his men had missed the First Manassas Campaign and were inexperienced. Their leader impressed his superiors during the operations around Yorktown. Promoted to major-general,

> **McLAWS' DIVISION**
> *Major-General Lafayette McLaws*
> **11 Staff and Field Officers**
>
> **Kershaw's Brigade 2,183**
> **Barksdale's Brigade 1,620**
> **Semmes' Brigade 1,334**
> **Wofford's Brigade 1,607**
> **Cabell's Artillery Battalion 378**

Major-General Lafayette McLaws, 42, was born in Georgia, had an undistinguished sojourn at West Point, and became a career soldier. Reliable and unimaginative, he took good care of his men.

McLaws led the Division into combat during the Seven Days' Battles at Savage's Station and Malvern Hill. When Lee reorganised the army, he assigned the Division to Longstreet's corps, thus beginning an association that would last for the next two years of almost constant campaigning.

The Division manned the Richmond defences during the Second Manassas Campaign. It participated in the Maryland Campaign with basically the same four infantry brigades and one artillery battalion that fought at Gettysburg. Its leader earned criticism from Lee when his division took 41 hours to march from Harper's Ferry to Sharpsburg at a time when Lee desperately needed manpower. Lee could not help but compare this performance to the nine hours A.P. Hill's Division required to complete the same march.

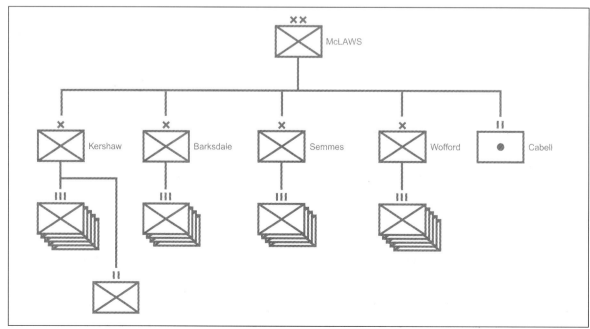

KERSHAW'S BRIGADE
Brigadier-General Joseph Brevard Kershaw
6 Staff and Field Officers

2nd South Carolina Volunteer Regiment
Colonel John Doby Kennedy
412 troops present for duty equipped

8th South Carolina Volunteer Regiment
Colonel John Williford Henagan
300 troops present for duty equipped

3rd South Carolina Volunteer Regiment
Major Robert Clayton Maffett
406 troops present for duty equipped

15th South Carolina Volunteer Regiment
Colonel William Davie de Saussure
448 troops present for duty equipped

7th South Carolina Volunteer Regiment
Lieutenant-Colonel Elbert Bland
408 troops present for duty equipped

3rd South Carolina Volunteer Battalion
Lieutenant-Colonel William George Rice
203 troops present for duty equipped

At Fredericksburg, McLaws' defensive preparations sheltered the Division when it manned a long trench behind a stone wall while its batteries occupied well-dug pits. From this position, the Division slaughtered the charging Federals at very little cost to themselves.

At Chancellorsville the Division blocked the Federal advance while Jackson performed his epic flank march. Then it counter-marched toward Fredericksburg to attack an isolated Union corps. Although McLaws was the most senior major-general in the army, his failure to show initiative and his deference to General Jubal Early robbed the Division of a great opportunity. Consequently, when Lee reorganised the army after Jackson's death, he passed over McLaws when promoting men to corps command.

The Division was well content to continue its association with McLaws. Although they made fun of his fussiness and rigidity in enforcing regulations by nick-

Brigadier-General Joseph Brevard Kershaw, a South Carolina lawyer and legislator, had served as a lieutenant in the Mexican War. He was 41 years old by the time he got to Gettysburg.

naming him "Make Laws", they appreciated his close attention to their needs off the battlefield and caution when using them in combat. By July 1863, McLaws and his Division had been together longer than anybody else in Lee's army.

Colonel Cabell's Artillery Battalion supported the Division. The Battalion was a thoroughly veteran outfit.

BARKSDALE'S BRIGADE
Brigadier-General William Barksdale
4 Staff and Field Officers

13th Mississippi Volunteer Infantry Regiment
Colonel James W. Carter
481 troops present for duty equipped

18th Mississippi Volunteer Infantry Regiment
Colonel Thomas M. Griffin
242 troops present for duty equipped

17th Mississippi Volunteer Infantry Regiment
Colonel William Dunbar Holder
469 troops present for duty equipped

21st Mississippi Volunteer Infantry Regiment
Colonel Benjamin Grubb Humphreys
424 troops present for duty equipped

SEMMES' BRIGADE
Brigadier-General Paul Jones Semmes
4 Staff and Field Officers

10th Regiment Georgia Volunteer Infantry
Colonel John B. Weems
303 troops present for duty equipped

51st Regiment Georgia Volunteer Infantry
Colonel Edward Ball
303 troops present for duty equipped

50th Regiment Georgia Volunteer Infantry
Colonel William R. Manning
302 troops present for duty equipped

53rd Regiment Georgia Volunteer Infantry
Colonel James Phillip Simms
422 troops present for duty equipped

WOFFORD'S BRIGADE
Brigadier-General William Tatum Wofford
4 Staff and Field Officers

16th Regiment Georgia Volunteer Infantry
Colonel Goode Bryan
303 troops present for duty equipped

Phillip's (Georgia) Legion Infantry
Lieutenant-Colonel Elihu Sandy Barclay, Jr.
273 troops present for duty equipped

18th Regiment Georgia Volunteer Infantry
Lieutenant-Colonel Solon Zackery Ruff
302 troops present for duty equipped

Cobb's (Georgia) Legion Infantry
Lieutenant-Colonel Luther Judson Glenn
213 troops present for duty equipped

24th Regiment Georgia Volunteer Infantry
Colonel Robert McMillan
303 troops present for duty equipped

Its batteries included the 1st Richmond Howitzers, which formed in 1859 and was the only Virginia unit in the Division. The Ellis Light Artillery formed in April 1861, while the two Georgia batteries both formed that autumn. July 1 found the Division at Greenwood, Pennsylvania, about 17 miles west of Gettysburg.

Divisional Artillery - Cabell's Battalion of Artillery
Colonel Henry Coalter Cabell
4 Staff and Field Officers

**Company A
10th North Carolina State Troops
Ellis Light Artillery**
Captain Basil Charles Manly
(131 troops present for duty equipped)
4 pieces

Pulaski Artillery (Georgia)
Captain John C. Fraser
(63 troops present for duty equipped)
4 pieces

Troup Artillery (Georgia)
Captain Henry H. Carlton
(90 troops present for duty equipped)
4 pieces

1st Richmond Howitzers (Virginia)
Captain Edward Stephens McCarthy
(90 troops present for duty equipped)
4 pieces

I CSA Army Corps - Pickett's Division

In February 1862 Brigadier-General George Pickett assumed command of a Virginia brigade that had been left leaderless when its commander,

Major-General George Edward Pickett, age 38 at Gettysburg, was last in his class at West Point. Undeterred, he became a career soldier whose meticulous attention to his grooming belied his hard-charging battlefield conduct.

Brigadier-General Philip Cocke, committed suicide. This brigade, which Richard Garnett would lead at Gettysburg, earned the nickname the "Game Cock Brigade" during the fighting at Williamsburg, Seven Pines, and Gaines' Mill. At Gaines' Mill Pickett suffered a shoulder wound that knocked him out of action for three months.

After reporting for duty in September 1862, Pickett received a sudden promotion to major-general. The promotion came because of Longstreet's friendship which dated back to the Mexican War.

Probably Longstreet was also repaying an emotional debt that had arisen when Pickett showed great kind-ness to Longstreet when that officer's children died the previous winter.

Initially the Division composed Pickett's old brigade commanded by Garnett, Kemper's Brigade, and a South Carolina Brigade commanded by Brigadier-General Jenkins. During the refit around Winchester, Virginia after the Sharpsburg Campaign, Armistead's Brigade joined the Division. November found the Division in the Fredericksburg area where Brigadier-General Corse's Brigade joined the Division. With this structure, the three brigades that were to march to Gettysburg - Garnett's, Kemper's, and Armistead's along with Dearing's four-battery artillery battalion - had formally taken their place. At Fredericksburg the Division was very lightly engaged and did not suffer a single fatality.

> **PICKETT'S DIVISION**
> *Major-General George Edward Pickett*
> **11 Staff and Field Officers**
>
> **Garnett's Brigade 1,459**
> **Kemper's Brigade 1,634**
> **Armistead's Brigade 1,950**
> **Dearing's Artillery Battalion 419**

Pickett's Division missed the Chancellorsville Campaign because it was on detached service with Longstreet. It endured a bleak ten-day march in snow

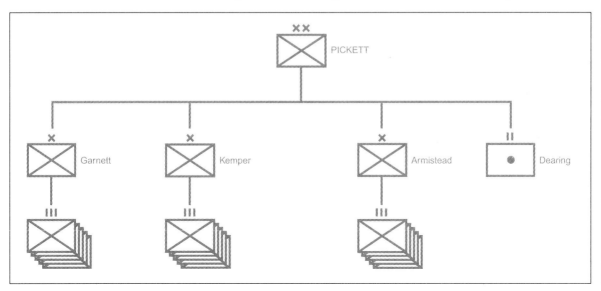

GARNETT'S BRIGADE
Brigadier-General Richard Brooke Garnett
4 Staff and Field Officers

8th Virginia Infantry Regiment
Colonel Eppa Hunton
193 troops present for duty equipped

18th Virginia Infantry Regiment
Lieutenant-Colonel Henry Alexander Carrington
312 troops present for duty equipped

19th Virginia Infantry Regiment
Colonel Henry Gantt
328 troops present for duty equipped

28th Virginia Infantry Regiment
Colonel Robert Clotworthy Allen
333 troops present for duty equipped

56th Virginia Infantry Regiment
Colonel William Dabney Stuart
289 troops present for duty equipped

and sleet to participate in the largely uneventful Suffolk Campaign. At this time many men were without shoes or blankets. Three brigades helped invest Suffolk while Garnett's and Kemper's Brigades went on foraging expeditions into eastern North Carolina. The Division's major combat occurred when a Federal amphibious operation captured all of the Fauquier Artillery with the exception of the drivers and battery horses. On the night of May 4, the Division withdrew from Suffolk and began its march to rejoin Lee's army.

Jenkins' Brigade remained on detached service while Corse's Brigade was detained at Hanover Junction to protect the railroads and bridges near Richmond. Thus, by the time of the Gettysburg Campaign, the Division had shrunk to a three-brigade unit. It was the only purely Virginia division in the Army of Northern

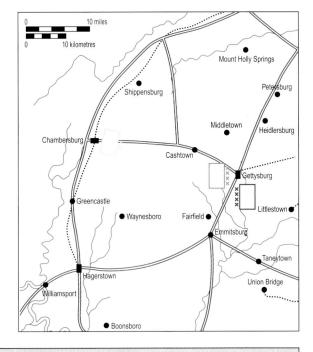

By the end of the first day's action at Gettysburg, Pickett's Division was still sitting 23 miles to the west at Chambersburg.

KEMPER'S BRIGADE
Brigadier-General James Lawson Kemper
4 Staff and Field Officers

1st Virginia Infantry Regiment
Colonel Lewis Burwell Williams, Jr.
209 troops present for duty equipped

3rd Virginia Infantry Regiment
Colonel Joseph Mayo, Jr.
332 troops present for duty equipped

7th Virginia Infantry Regiment
Colonel Waller Tazewell Patton
335 troops present for duty equipped

11th Virginia Infantry Regiment
Major Kirkwood Otey
359 troops present for duty equipped

24th Virginia Infantry Regiment
Colonel William Richard Terry
395 troops present for duty equipped

Virginia. Although its components were battle-tested, it did not have much experience as a division under Pickett's leadership.

The quality of that leadership was an open question. Long after Pickett's promotion, Longstreet's aide, Moxley Sorrel, referred to him sarcastically as a "good brigadier." Sorrel would write that Longstreet would carefully issue very complete orders to Pickett and instruct his aides to "give him things very fully; indeed,

Battle flag of Major John Owen's 9th Virginia Infantry Regiment.

ARMISTEAD'S BRIGADE
Brigadier-General Lewis Addison Armistead
4 Staff and Field Officers

9th Virginia Infantry Regiment
Major John Crowder Owens
257 troops present for duty equipped

53rd Virginia Infantry Regiment
Colonel William Roane Aylett
435 troops present for duty equipped

14th Virginia Infantry Regiment
Colonel James Gregory Hodges
422 troops present for duty equipped

38th Virginia Infantry Regiment
Colonel Edward Claxton Edmonds
356 troops present for duty equipped

57th Virginia Infantry Regiment
Colonel John Bowie Magruder
476 troops present for duty equipped

Divisional Artillery - 38th Battalion of Virginia Light Artillery
Major James Dearing
9 Staff and Field Officers

Company A
Fauquier Artillery (Virginia)
Captain Robert Mackey Stribling
(134 troops present for duty equipped)
4 pieces

Company B
Richmond Fayette Artillery (Virginia)
Captain Miles Cary Macon
(90 troops present for duty equipped)
4 pieces

Company C
Hampden Artillery (Virginia)
Captain William Henderson Caskie
(90 troops present for duty equipped)
4 pieces

Company D
Lynchburg Artillery (Virginia)
Captain Joseph Grey Blount
(96 troops present for duty equipped)
4 pieces

Brigadier-General Lewis Addison Armistead, a battle-field elder at 46, was thrown out of West Point. However, he persevered in his ambition to become a career soldier in the tradition of his family.

sometimes stay with him to make sure he did not get astray."

On June 27 the Division camped outside of Chambersburg, Pennsylvania. Here it worked at destroying railroad depots, workshops, and public machinery while guarding the army's rear. It remained near Chambersburg until relieved by Brigadier-General John Imboden's cavalry brigade. Since Imboden was late to arrive, the Division did not receive orders to march to Gettysburg until late in the evening of July 1.

I CSA Army Corps - Hood's Division

The army had no more famous division than that commanded by John B. Hood. The Division revelled in the fact that outside of Lee himself, their leader, with his unequaled combat record, enjoyed the greatest admiration among the Southern people in the summer of 1863.

Major-General John Bell Hood at 32 was a bachelor adored by women and a fierce fighting general idolised by his men. At West Point he was an undistinguished cadet, but became a career soldier rather than the Kentucky doctor his family expected.

The Division began its association with Hood during the Peninsula Campaign. When Hood, at the head of his brigade, led a charge that broke the Federal line at Gaines' Mill, it earned both him and his men renown as the fiercest assault troops in Lee's army. As a reward, during the post-Campaign reorganisation, Lee promoted Hood to divisional command.

The two-brigade Division enhanced its reputation at Second Manassas when it spearheaded Longstreet's crushing assault that nearly destroyed Pope's Federal army. At the Battle of South Mountain during the Maryland Campaign of 1862, the men showed their respect for their leader. He was under arrest and riding at the rear of the Division. As the Division marched toward the fight they began to yell, "Give us Hood!" Lee responded, "You shall have him, gentlemen!"

HOOD'S DIVISION
Major-General John Bell Hood
11 Staff and Field Officers

Law's Brigade 1,933
Anderson's Brigade 1,874
Robertson's Brigade 1,734
Benning's Brigade 1,420
Henry's Artillery Battalion 403

The Division followed its charismatic leader at Sharpsburg to deliver an impetuous, but extremely costly counterattack to seal a breach in Lee's lines. According to Hood, here it experienced "the most terrible clash of arms, by far" of the entire war.

Fredericksburg found the Division expanded to four brigades and its leader promoted to major-general at the recommendation of "Stonewall" Jackson. The two Georgia brigades that joined the Division were veteran outfits led by respected officers. The Division occupied a quiet sector at that battle, losing fewer than 400 men. It missed the carnage at Chancellorsville when it was

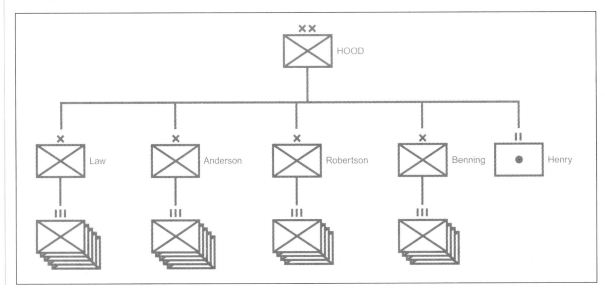

LAW'S BRIGADE
Brigadier-General Evander McIvor Law
4 Staff and Field Officers

4th Alabama Infantry Regiment
Lieutenant-Colonel
Lawrence Houston Scruggs
346 troops present for duty equipped

47th Alabama Infantry Regiment
Colonel James W. Jackson
347 troops present for duty equipped

15th Alabama Infantry Regiment
Colonel William Calvin Oates
499 troops present for duty equipped

44th Alabama Infantry Regiment
Colonel William Flake Perry
363 troops present for duty equipped

48th Alabama Infantry Regiment
Colonel James Lawrence Sheffield
374 troops present for duty equipped

detached to participate in Longstreet's Suffolk Campaign in southeastern Virginia.

Henry's four-battery artillery battalion provided fire support for the Division. The German Artillery was raised before the war in Charleston. True to its German roots, its men initially wore Prussian-style helmets for dress parade. Its sister Charleston battery, the Palmetto Light Artillery, was less experienced, having formed in the spring of 1862. The two North Carolina batteries, the Branch and Rowan artillery, formed in January 1862 and May 1861, respectively.

The Division entered the Gettysburg Campaign in high spirits. It had not endured stiff combat since

Brigadier-General Evander McIvor Law, a 26-year-old from South Carolina, graduated from the forerunner to The Citadel and founded a military academy in Alabama. At the outbreak of the war, he raised a company from among his students.

ANDERSON'S BRIGADE
Brigadier-General George Thomas Anderson
10 Staff and Field Officers

7th Regiment Georgia Volunteer Infantry
Colonel William Wilkinson White
377 troops present for duty equipped

11th Regiment Georgia Volunteer Infantry
Colonel Francis H. Little
310 troops present for duty equipped

8th Regiment Georgia Volunteer Infantry
Colonel John R. Towers
312 troops present for duty equipped

9th Regiment Georgia Volunteer Infantry
Lieutenant-Colonel John C. Mounger
340 troops present for duty equipped

59th Regiment Georgia Volunteer Infantry
Colonel William A. Jackson Brown
525 troops present for duty equipped

I CSA Corps Reserve Artillery

Colonel Walton's two-battalion artillery reserve came into existence following Lee's reorganisation of the army after the 1862 Seven Days' Battles. The same ten batteries served together at Second Manassas, Sharpsburg, Fredericksburg and Chancellorsville. Thus, they had wide, cooperative experience. The Reserve also enjoyed fine commanders. At Gettysburg, Walton served as Chief of Artillery

---

I ARMY CORPS RESERVE ARTILLERY
Colonel James Burdge Walton
4 Staff and Field Officers

---

for the entire I Corps. The Reserve's two battalion commanders were equally able, experienced artillerymen.

Alexander's six-battery battalion composed batteries from three different states and thus unlike its sister battalion had no pre-war unit association. Prominent among them was the Madison Light Artillery, the "Madison Tips," organised in May 1861, the Brooks Light Artillery raised in Charleston in 1862, and Parker's Battery formed in Richmond in 1862.

Eshleman's Washington Artillery was one of the most famed artillery units in the entire Confederacy. Organised in New Orleans in 1838, it had long attracted the city's prominent citizens. It went to war superbly drilled and outfitted, with its members dressed in dark blue frock coats and sky blue trousers, red kepis, and white canvas gaiters. At Gettysburg probably only the officers retained this uniform.

During the march through Pennsylvania, the reserve enjoyed living off of the 'fat' of the land. However, the men and horses endured excessive heat, dry weather and dust during the march to Gettysburg. Porter's Battalion reached the field at 0900 on July 2 while Eshleman's battalion arrived late that evening.

Washington Artillery Battalion (Louisiana)
Major Benjamin Franklin Eshleman
9 Staff and Field Officers

1st Company
Captain Charles W. Squires
(77 troops present for duty equipped)
1 piece

2nd Company
Captain John B. Richardson
(80 troops present for duty equipped)
3 pieces

3rd Company
Captain Merritt B. Miller
(92 troops present for duty equipped)
3 12-pounder Napoleon guns

4th Company
Captain Joseph Norcom
(80 troops present for duty equipped)
3 pieces

Alexander's Battalion of Artillery
Colonel Edward Porter Alexander
9 Staff and Field Officers

Ashland Light Artillery (Virginia)
Captain Pichegru Woolfolk, Jr.
(103 troops present for duty equipped)
4 pieces

Bedford Light Artillery (Virginia)
Captain Tyler Calhoun Jordan
(78 troops present for duty equipped)
4 pieces

Brooks Artillery (South Carolina)
Lieutenant S. Capers Gilbert
(71 troops present for duty equipped)
4 pieces

Madison Light Artillery (Louisiana)
Captain George V. Moody
(135 troops present for duty equipped)
4 pieces

Captain William Watts Parker's Company
Virginia Light Artillery
Captain William Watts Parker
(90 troops present for duty equipped)
4 pieces

Captain Osmond B. Taylor's Company
Virginia Light Artillery
Captain Osmond B. Taylor
(90 troops present for duty equipped)
4 pieces

THE ARMY OF NORTHERN VIRGINIA

II CSA Army Corps

II Corps, like its sister I Corps, came into existence in 1862 when Lee reorganised the army after the Seven Days' Battles.

Under the command of Thomas "Stonewall" Jackson it achieved enduring renown for its hard, fast marching and lightning battlefield strokes. The shocking loss of its commander at Chancellorsville required the Corps

Lieutenant-General Richard Stoddert Ewell. His II Corps had reached Carlisle where he was ordered to concentrate at Gettysburg. Ewell turned south and arrived on the battlefield at about 1430 hrs on July 1st, just in time to strike the Federals in the flank and force a retreat.

to adjust to both a new commander and a modified organisation.

The eccentric Richard Ewell, recovered from his leg amputation caused by a wound at Second Manassas and newly promoted to lieutenant-general, took charge

---

II CORPS
Lieutenant-General
Richard Stoddert Ewell

Early's Division
Major-General Jubal Anderson Early
Johnson's Division
Major-General Edward Johnson
Rodes' Division
Major-General Robert Emmett Rodes
II Corps Reserve Artillery
Colonel John Thompson Brown

---

17 Staff and Field Officers

Escort/Couriers
39th Battalion Virginia Cavalry
Captain William F. Randolph
31 troops present for duty equipped

Co. B Captain William F. Randolph's Co.

Provost Guard
Cos. A and B, 1st Battalion
North Carolina Sharpshooters
Major Rufus Watson Wharton
94 troops present for duty equipped

---

of the Corps. The men knew and liked "old Bald Head." He had been Jackson's most trusted subordinate during the celebrated Valley Campaign of 1862. The Corps lost A.P. Hill's so-called Light Division and Colquitt's Georgia Brigade.

Among the remaining three divisions, only Jubal Early's stayed intact. Divisional commands went to Edward Johnson, who was returning to duty after a year-long absence spent recovering from a wound, and to Robert Rodes, who ascended from brigade to divisional command. New to the Corps was Daniel's North Carolina Brigade in Rodes' Division.

June 30 found the Corps scattered with Johnson's Division northeast of Chambersburg and Rodes and Early between Carlisle and Gettysburg.

II CSA Corps Casualties
at Gettysburg
1st July 1863

Infantry killed or wounded	2,574
Infantry missing/captured	848
Artillery killed or wounded	50
Artillery missing/captured	0

II CSA ARMY CORPS - GETTYSBURG - July 1

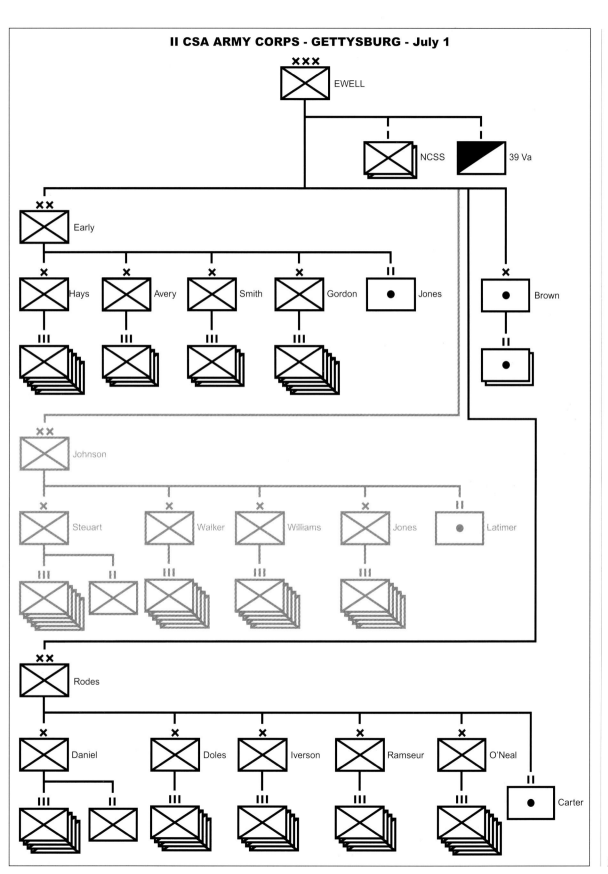

EWELL

NCSS

39 Va

Early

Hays

Avery

Smith

Gordon

Jones

Brown

Johnson

Steuart

Walker

Williams

Jones

Latimer

Rodes

Daniel

Doles

Iverson

Ramseur

O'Neal

Carter

II CSA Army Corps - Early's Division

Early's Division knew and respected its commander. Their association dated back to the time when Early's Virginia Brigade had served in Ewell's Division. The Division saw Early rise to temporary command on the field at Sharpsburg. According to Stonewall Jackson, the Division both held its position and "attacked with great vigor and gallantry." Lee commended Early's performance and rewarded him with the assignment of divisional commander.

At Fredericksburg Early's Division counterattacked Meade's penetration. The men charged at the run shouting, "Here comes old Jubal! Let old Jubal straighten out that fence!"

After Early received a promotion to major-general in April 1863, the Division, which up to that time was still called "Ewell's Division", was permanently placed in Early's hands.

EARLY'S DIVISION
Major-General Jubal Anderson Early
12 Staff and Field Officers

Hays' Brigade 1,295
Hoke's (Avery's) Brigade 1,244
Smith's Brigade 806
Gordon's Brigade 1,813
Jones' Artillery Battalion 290

Major-General Jubal Anderson Early, 46 and afflicted with rheumatism, was disliked and unlikeable by all but Lee. The Virginian lawyer and legislator had turned in a respectable performance at West Point.

During the Chancellorsville Campaign, the Division received the difficult mission to hold the Fredericksburg lines while the balance of the army marched to engage Hooker's army in the Wilderness.

Over-stretched, the Division lost its ground but recovered to help drive the Union VI Corps across the river. The Division lost more than 800 men during the campaign.

The Gettysburg Campaign found the Division assigned to Ewell's restructured II Corps and Early in the familiar position as Ewell's subordinate. Given Ewell's generous, agreeable nature and Early's overbearing, independent attitude, there was a potential for confusion regarding lines of authority. However, the Division's smashing success at the Battle of Winchester on June 14, was a victory worthy of Jackson himself, and indicated that all should be well for the future of the Division.

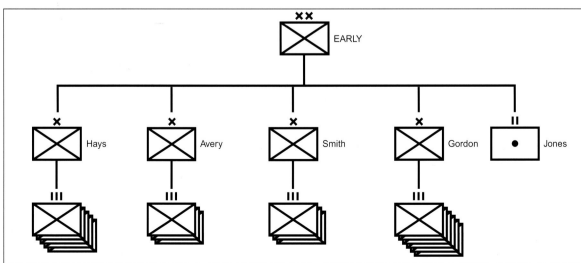

Early's Division - Hays' Brigade

Brigadier-General Harry Hays began his association with Louisiana soldiers when he became Colonel of the 7th Louisiana, the so-called Pelican Regiment, named for the white pelican prominently displayed on the regimental colours. According to army commander General Pierre T. Beauregard, he led the 7th at First Manassas with "satisfactory coolness and skill."

The following year the Pelican Regiment merged with the 6th, 8th, and 9th Louisiana regiments as well as Wheat's Battalion to form an all-Louisiana brigade commanded by Richard Taylor. The Brigade distinguished itself during Stonewall Jackson's Valley Campaign and Hays received a bullet wound in the shoulder at the Battle of Port Republic on June 9, 1862. Taylor was promoted and transferred to the

> ### HAYS' BRIGADE
> ### *Brigadier-General Harry Thompson Hays*
> ### 3 Staff and Field Officers

With Jubal Early now commanding the Division, at Chancellorsville Hays' Brigade helped defend the extensive Fredericksburg lines. It joined the Division's retreat when confronted with the Federal VI Corps' overwhelming force on May 3, 1863. It had the satisfaction of participating in the savage attacks that drove VI Corps back over the Rappahannock the next day. The charge cost the brigade 370 casualties. When Early saw Hays' Brigade pierce the Union lines, he threw down his hat and exclaimed, "Those Louisiana fellows can steal as much as they please now!"

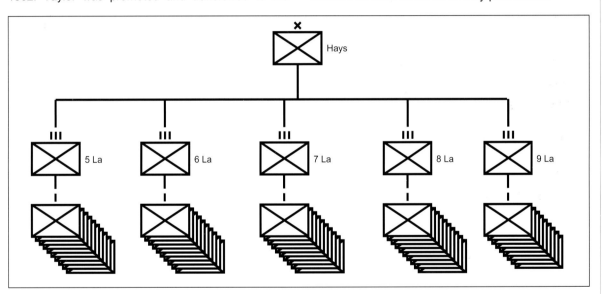

Trans-Mississippi. The Brigade received a newly promoted Hays to replace him.

The 5th Louisiana joined the Brigade for the Sharpsburg Campaign while Wheat's Battalion - the original "Louisiana Tigers" - was broken up with its manpower distributed to the other regiments. Under Hays' command, the Brigade fought at Sharpsburg where in excess of half its men became casualties during the fighting in the Cornfield.

The Brigade assumed the structure it was to take north to Gettysburg by December 1862. Serving in Ewell's Division at Fredericksburg it was only lightly engaged, suffering a total of 55 casualties.

> ### 5th Louisiana Infantry Regiment
> ### *Major Alexander Hart*
> ### 196 troops present for duty equipped
>
> Co. A **Crescent City Guards**
> Co. B **Chalmette Rifle Guards**
> Co. C **Bienville Guards**
> Co. D **DeSoto Rifles**
> Co. E **Orleans Cadet Co.**
> Co. F **Orleans Southrons**
> Co. G **Louisiana Swamp Rangers**
> Co. H **Perret Guards**
> Co. I   **Carondelet Invincibles**
> Co. K **Monroe Guards**

6th Louisiana Infantry Regiment
Lieutenant-Colonel Joseph Hanlon
218 troops present for duty equipped

Co. A Union and Sabine Guards
Co. B Calhoun Guards
Co. C St. Landry Light Guards
Co. D Tensas Rifles
Co. E Mercer Guards
Co. F Irish Brigade Co.
Co. G Pemberton Rangers
Co. H Orleans Rifles
Co. I Irish Brigade Co. A
Co. K Violet Guards

8th Louisiana Infantry Regiment
Colonel Trevanion D. Lewis
296 troops present for duty equipped

Co. A Creole Guards
Co. B Bienville Rifles
Co. C Attakapas Guards
Co. D Sumter Guards
Co. E Franklin Sharpshooters
Co. F Opelousas Guards
Co. G Minden Blues
Co. H Cheneyville Rifles
Co. I Rapides Invincibles
Co. K Phoenix Co.

Brigadier-General Harry Thompson Hays, 43 years old, was raised in Mississippi and practiced law in New Orleans. His only previous military experience had been in the Mexican War, but he was able to handle a tough band of Louisianans.

Battle flag, claimed to be that of the 8th Louisiana Infantry Regiment, captured at Rappahannock Station in November 1863.

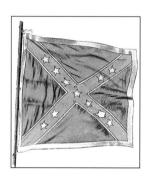

From the time of their arrival in Virginia, Louisiana troops as a whole suffered a bad reputation for drunkenness, poor discipline, desertion, and pillaging. Much of this reputation stemmed from the behaviour of Wheat's and Coppens' battalions and a general prejudice against foreigners. The vast majority of the 5th Louisiana were labourers and clerks with about two-fifths of the total foreign born. The 6th, known as the 'Irish Brigade', had the highest percentage of foreign-born members at 54%. The 7th, described by Richard Taylor as a "crack" regiment, had about one-third of its men born in Louisiana and one-third in Ireland. The 8th, comprised mostly of farmers and labourers, had soldiers born in at least eighteen foreign countries with a conspicuous Creole component. The 9th had the largest percentage of native-born Louisiana soldiers and was to have three brigadier-generals promoted from its officer corps.

No one questioned the Louisiana soldiers' toughness. Hays himself was also tough enough to control them. On the eve of the Gettysburg Campaign, Hays and his brigade had been together for ten months and established a hard-hitting reputation.

7th Louisiana Infantry Regiment
Colonel Davidson Bradfute Penn
235 troops present for duty equipped

Co. A Continental Guards
Co. B Baton Rouge Fencibles
Co. C Sarsfield Rangers
Co. D Virginia Guards
Co. E Crescent City Rifles Co. B
Co. F Irish Volunteers
Co. G American Rifles
Co. H Crescent City Rifles Co. C
Co. I Virginia Blues
Co. K Livingston Rifles

9th Louisiana Infantry Regiment
Colonel Leroy Augustus Stafford
347 troops present for duty equipped

Co. A Moore Fencibles
Co. B Stafford Guides
Co. C Bienville Blues
Co. D Bossier Volunteers
Co. E Milliken Bend Guards
Co. F DeSoto Blues
Co. G Colyell Guards
Co. H Brush Valley Guards
Co. I Washington Rifles

Early's Division - Hoke's (Avery's) Brigade

Hoke's North Carolina Brigade composed three veteran combat units. Two of them had long service records and had contributed officers to the army's higher command echelon. The 6th North Carolina State Troops formed in Charlotte in May 1861. It fought at First Manassas in Bee's Brigade where one of its captains, Isaac Avery, received a wound. At one time, William D. Pender had been its colonel.

When he was promoted, Avery, who had fought with the regiment at Seven Pines, became the 6th's colonel. An officer observed that "there was no fall back in Avery," a point proven again when Avery received a severe wound at Gaines' Mill. The regiment's ferocious combat ability earned it the nickname "the Bloody Sixth."

The 21st North Carolina Troops, initially called the 11th Regiment, formed in Danville, Virginia in June 1861 and fought with Bonham's Brigade at First Manassas. Before promotion to Brigadier-General, Robert Hoke had been the unit's colonel. In contrast, the 57th North Carolina Troops formed in July 1862. Its introduction to combat came at Fredericksburg. On that field the 21st served in Trimble's Brigade, which became Hoke's command, while the 6th and 57th served in Law's Brigade of Hood's Division.

The 6th North Carolina transferred to Hoke's Brigade in January 1863. Colonel Avery, who had recovered from his wound, returned that spring to command.

HOKE'S (AVERY'S) BRIGADE
Colonel Isaac Erwin Avery/
Colonel Archibald Campbell Godwin
2 Staff and Field Officers

For the first time, during the Chancellorsville Campaign the three regiments served together in the same brigade along with two other North Carolina units. As part of Early's Division, it defended the Fredericksburg position on May 3 and participated in the May 4 assault against Sedgwick. The Brigade suffered 230 casualties during the campaign. When Hoke received a serious wound, Colonel Avery assumed command. He was a strict disciplinarian and impress-

---

6th North Carolina State Troops
Major Samuel McDowell Tate
509 troops present for duty equipped

Co. A *Name not available*
Co. B *Name not available*
Co. C *Name not available*
Co. D *Name not available*
Co. E *Name not available*
Co. F *Name not available*
Co. G *Name not available*
Co. H **Caswell Boys**
Co. I **Cedar Fork Rifles**
Co. K *Name not available*

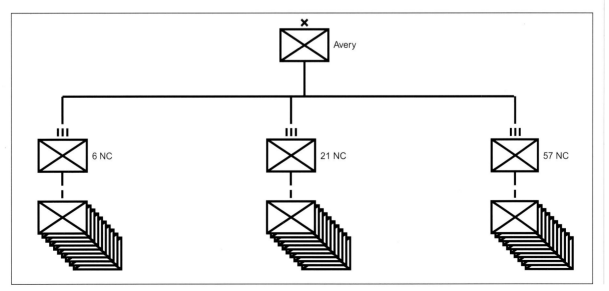

21st Regiment North Carolina Troops
Colonel William Whedbee Kirkland
436 troops present for duty equipped

Co. A   Davidson Guards
Co. C   Blue Ridge Riflemen
Co. D   Forsyth Rifles
Co. F   Mountain Boys
Co. G   Town Fork Invincibles
Co. H   Mountain Tigers
Co. I   Surry Marksmen
Co. K   Forsyth Southrons
Co. L   Rockingham Invincibles
Co. M Guilford Dixie Boys

57th Regiment North Carolina Troops
Colonel Archibald Campbell Godwin
297 troops present for duty equipped

Cos. A thru K. *All Company names not available*

ed his superiors including Pender, Hood, and Early. Lee however considered him unready for promotion to General.

The Brigade departed the Fredericksburg lines around 2300 hours on June 4. It participated in the combats around Winchester beginning on June 13 but was not heavily engaged losing only one killed and three wounded. However, the Brigade was weakened when General Early detached the Brigade's 54th North Carolina and ordered it to guard the Federal prisoners captured at Winchester. The Brigade's 1st Battalion North Carolina Sharpshooters was also detached to serve as provost guard for II Corps.

The Brigade crossed the Potomac near Sheperdstown on June 22. As it passed through York, Pennsylvania, curious onlookers gathered and a child asked, "Why Papa I thought the Rebs had horns, where are they?" The soldiers brandished their bayonets and replied, "Here are our horns!"

Early's Division - Smith's Brigade

Brigadier-General William Smith first commanded the Brigade at Sharpsburg when he replaced Early who had risen to divisional command. At Sharpsburg it composed seven Virginia regiments, three of which were to form the brigade Smith commanded at Gettysburg. The Virginians admired Smith's courage. Although he suffered three wounds at Sharpsburg, he stayed on the field. They

SMITH'S BRIGADE
Brigadier-General William Smith
4 Staff and Field Officers

thought less of his tactical prowess. At Chancellorsville his deployments were awkward and the Brigade's performance second-rate.

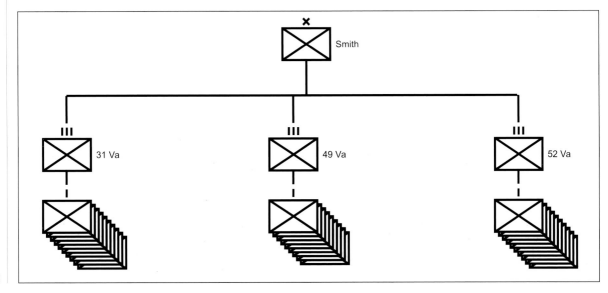

31st Virginia Infantry Regiment
Colonel John Stringer Hoffman
267 troops present for duty equipped

Co. A   Marion Guard
Co. B   Captain Robert H. Bradshaw's Co.
Co. C   Captain Uriel M. Turner's Co.
Co. D   Gilmer Rifles
Co. E   The Highlanders
Co. F   Captain Jacob Currence's Co.
Co. G   Captain James C. Arbogast's Co.
Co. H   Captain Albert G. Reger's Co.
Co. I   Captain Alfred H. Jackson's Co.
Co. K   Captain Henry Sturn's Co.

49th Virginia Infantry Regiment
Lieutenant-Colonel Jonathan Catlett Gibson
281 troops present for duty equipped

Co. A   Ewell Guards
Co. B   Quantico Guards
Co. C   Fauquier Guards
Co. D   Warren Blues
Co. E   Flint Hill Rifles
Co. F   Captain William H. Crowder's Co.
Co. H   New Market Volunteers
Co. I   Amherst Rough and Readys
Co. K   Sperryville Sharp Shooters

Smith personally led the march when the Brigade entered York, Pennsylvania. As a former member of the Confederate Congress he could not resist the opportunity to perform. He removed his hat and saluted the girls "with that manly, hearty smile which no man or woman ever doubted or resisted."

As much as the brigade enjoyed their colourful commander, they recognised his deficiencies. Reputedly he received a heavy vote from the army in Virginia's gubernatorial race because the Brigade wished to get rid of him. Early tried to keep the Brigade united with John Gordon's Brigade so Smith could benefit from Gordon's military wisdom.

52nd Virginia Infantry Regiment
Lieutenant-Colonel James H. Skinner
254 troops present for duty equipped

Co. A   Augusta Fencibles
Co. B   Captain William Long's Co.
Co. C   Letcher Guard
Co. D   Captain Joseph F. Hottel's Co.
Co. E   Captain Thomas H. Watkin's Co.
Co. F   Captain Joseph E. Cline's Co.
Co. G   Captain Samuel McCune's Co.
Co. H   Staunton Pioneers
Co. I   Men of West Augusta
Co. K   Captain Benjamin J. Walton's Co.

Early's Division - Gordon's Brigade

The association between the six Georgia regiments and their brigadier began in April 1863 when Gordon returned after a seven month convalescence to take temporary command of Lawton's Brigade. During the Chancellorsville Campaign, the Brigade received the assignment to retake Marye's

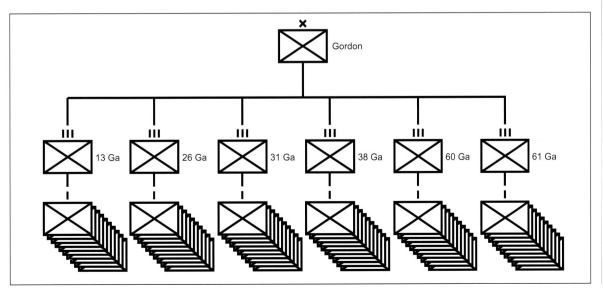

GORDON'S BRIGADE
Brigadier-General John Brown Gordon
6 Staff and Field Officers

Brigadier-General John Brown Gordon, age 31, was a lawyer from Georgia. Accompanied on campaign throughout the war by his wife, when she went to the rear, his men knew that battle was imminent.

13th Regiment Georgia Volunteer Infantry
Colonel James Milton Smith
312 troops present for duty equipped

Co. A Confederate Guards
Co. B Meriwether Volunteers
Co. C Ringgold Rangers
Co. D Upson Volunteers
Co. E Randolph Volunteers
Co. F Fayette Rangers
Co. G Early Guards
Co. H Panola Rifles
Co. I   Stark Volunteers
Co. K Evans Guards

Heights. According to a soldier in the 13th Georgia, Gordon said, "Wait until you get up close to the heights. Let every man raise a yell and take those heights...Will you do it? I ask you to go no farther than I am willing to lead!" Such inspirational leadership

26th Regiment Georgia Volunteer Infantry
Colonel Edmund Nathan Atkinson
315 troops present for duty equipped

Co. A Brunswick Riflemen
Co. B McIntosh County Guards
Co. C Piscola Volunteers
Co. D Seaboard Guards
Co. E Wiregrass Minute Men
Co. F Ware Guards
Co. G Okefenokee Rifles
Co. H Bartow Light Infantry
Co. I   Faulk Invincibles
Co. K Forest Rangers

31st Regiment Georgia Volunteer Infantry
Colonel Clement Anselm Evans
252 troops present for duty equipped

Co. A Georgia Light Infantry
Co. B Muscogee Confederates
Co. C Mitchell Guards
Co. D Monroe Crowders
Co. E Bartow Guards
Co. F Pulaski Blues
Co. G *Name not available*
Co. H Mountain Tigers
Co. I   Arnet Rifles
Co. K Bartow Avengers

completely won over the Brigade. As another veteran recalled, Gordon was "the most prettiest thing you ever did see on a field of fight." He would "put fight into a whipped chicken just to look at him."

Before the Gettysburg Campaign, the Brigade's officers unanimously petitioned that Gordon remain in command. One officer added the condition that Gordon not address them before they went into battle.

38th Regiment Georgia Volunteer Infantry
Captain William L. McLeod
341 troops present for duty equipped

Co. A Murphey Guards
Co. B Milton Guards
Co. C Ben Hill Guards
Co. D McCullough Rifles
Co. E Tom Cobb Infantry
Co. F Thornton Volunteers
Co. G Batley Guards
Co. H Goshen Blues
Co. I   Irwin Invincibles
Co. K Bartow Avengers

When asked why, he replied, "Because he makes me feel like I could storm hell."

On June 13, 1863, the Brigade joined in the combat at Winchester, Virginia where it charged a Federal battery. Gordon reported, "In this charge, which was executed with spirit and unchecked at any point, my brigade lost 75 men, including some efficient officers."

The Brigade was detached from the Division and advanced to the Susquehanna River near Wrightsville where it encountered a large body of Pennsylvania militia. The Brigade drove the militia over the river and then rejoined the Division. On June 30 it was camped near Heidlersburg, northeast of Gettysburg.

60th Regiment Georgia Volunteer Infantry
Captain Waters Burras Jones
299 troops present for duty equipped

Co. A Anthony Grays
Co. B Fannin Guards
Co. C Walker Independents
Co. D Whitfield Volunteers
Co. E Bartow Avengers
Co. F Gilmer Volunteers
Co. G Dooly Guards
Co. H *Name not available*
Co. I *Name not available*
Co. K *Name not available*

61st Regiment Georgia Volunteer Infantry
Colonel John Hill Lamar
288 troops present for duty equipped

Co. A Irwin Cowboys
Co. B Tattnall Rangers
Co. C Wiregrass Rifles
Co. D DeKalb Guards
Co. E Montgomery Sharpshooters
Co. F Stark Guards
Co. G Wilkes Guards
Co. H Tattnall County Volunteers
Co. I Thompson Guards
Co. K *Name not available*

Early's Division - Jones' Artillery Battalion

Jones' Artillery Battalion began the campaign under strength, taking only thirteen artillery pieces on the march from Fredericksburg.

At the Battle of Winchester, June 14, 1863, the Battalion made a circuitous, 10-mile march to obtain a commanding position overlooking a Union fortification. After Jones carefully reconnoitred the ground, he positioned his own battalion and two batteries from

The 3-inch ordnance rifle was favoured for its manoeuverability and accuracy at long range. It fired a 10-pound shell more than 2,000 yards.

Dance's Battalion in favourable locations just behind the crest line. On signal the guns moved forward and opened a telling fire. After the artillery obtained fire superiority, the infantry charged. The entire operation was typical of the Battalion's training, featuring careful preparation, thorough reconnaissance, and fine front-line leadership by Jones and his battery officers. The infantry captured six 3-inch rifled cannon.

Divisional Artillery
Lieutenant-Colonel Hilary Pollard Jones
9 Staff and Field Officers

This allowed the Battalion to add captured Federal pieces to bring it up to its authorised strength of sixteen guns, with Green's Louisiana Guard Artillery gaining two Union rifled guns.

Jones' Battalion of Artillery

Charlottesville Artillery (Virginia)
Captain James McDowell Carrington
(71 troops present for duty equipped)
4 12-pounder Napoleon guns

Courtney Artillery (Virginia)
Captain William A. Tanner
(90 troops present for duty equipped)
4 3-inch rifled guns

Louisiana Guard Battery
Captain Charles A. Green
(60 troops present for duty equipped)
2 3-inch rifled guns
2 10-pounder Parrott rifled guns

Staunton Artillery (Virginia)
Captain Asher Waterman Garber
(60 troops present for duty equipped)
4 12-pounder Napoleon guns

II CSA Army Corps - Johnson's Division

The unit that was to become Johnson's Division had formerly been "Stonewall" Jackson's own command. It contained the heart of Jackson's Valley Army. Since those glory days it had had a succession of temporary commanders.

It was led at Cedar Mountain by Brigadier-General Charles Winder. When Winder fell to Federal artillery fire, Brigadier-General William Taliaferro replaced him. Taliaferro commanded at Second Manassas where he was wounded. At Sharpsburg the Division, led by

> **JOHNSON'S DIVISION**
> *Major-General Edward Johnson*
> **9 Staff and Field Officers**
>
> **Steuart's Brigade 2,121**
> **Stonewall (Walker's) Brigade 1,323**
> **Nicholl's (Williams') Brigade 1,104**
> **Jones' Brigade 1,467**
> **Latimer's Artillery Battalion 356**

Major-General Edward Johnson, after a mediocre West Point sojourn, served in the Mexican War and on the frontier. However, at 47, he had relatively little experience of battle.

Brigadier-General John Jones - an officer who was to command one of the Division's brigades at Gettysburg - bore the brunt of the first Federal attack and suffered fearfully.

The Division was lightly engaged at Fredericksburg where a recovered Taliaferro again commanded. Following Taliaferro's transfer (Jackson had never liked him) the Division was led by Brigadier-General Raleigh Colston. During the Chancellorsville Campaign, the Division participated in Jackson's flank march and deployed as the second wave for his devastating attack, but suffered 2,090 infantry casualties during the battle. However Lee was displeased with Colston's leadership, sent him to Georgia and summoned Major-General Edward Johnson to replace him.

The Division's new commander had suffered a bad ankle wound at the Battle of McDowell in May 1862. It took a full year to heal and thus Johnson missed the Army of Northern Virginia's formative battles. But his conduct had attracted Stonewall Jackson's favourable

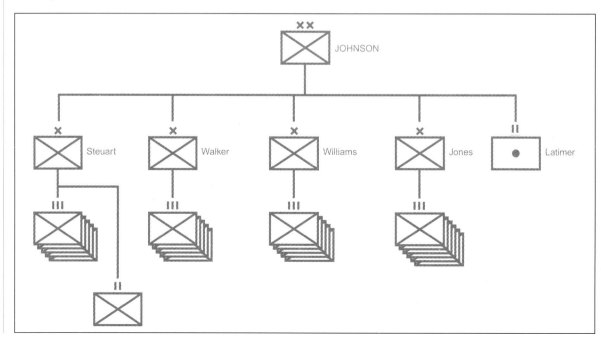

STEUART'S BRIGADE
Brigadier-General George Hume Steuart
5 Staff and Field Officers

1st Maryland Battalion Infantry
Lieutenant-Colonel James R. Herbert
400 troops present for duty equipped

1st North Carolina State Troops
Lieutenant-Colonel Hamilton Allen Brown
377 troops present for duty equipped

3rd North Carolina State Troops
Major William Murdoch Parsley
548 troops present for duty equipped

10th Virginia Infantry Regiment
Colonel Edward Tiffin Harrison Warren
276 troops present for duty equipped

23rd Virginia Infantry Regiment
Lieutenant-Colonel Simeon Taylor Walton
251 troops present for duty equipped

37th Virginia Infantry Regiment
Major Henry Clinton Wood
264 troops present for duty equipped

attention. Jackson had wanted Johnson as one of his divisional commanders. It was a particularly poignant request given the presence of the famous "Stonewall Brigade" in the division. However, when Johnson took command he was the only divisional commander who was a complete newcomer to the army.

Three of his four brigade commanders were also leading their brigades into combat for the first time, while, Jones, the fourth, was widely suspected of cowardice and incompetence.

Johnson's service in the Allegheny mountains had earned him the nickname "Old Allegheny." The Division quickly dubbed him "Old Clubby" because he walked with the aid of a heavy hickory staff. His habit of swearing at and hitting skulkers with his stick did not enhance his popularity. Soldiers called him a "brute" and one of the "wickedest men I have ever heard of."

The Division departed its camps near Fredericks-

The tattered flag of the 2nd Virginia Infantry Regiment carries the battle honour 'Gettysburg' and was captured later in the war.

Battle flag of Major William Terry's 4th Virginia Infantry Regiment, captured at the Battle of the Wilderness, 1864.

STONEWALL (WALKER'S) BRIGADE
Brigadier-General James Alexander Walker
4 Staff and Field Officers

2nd Virginia Infantry Regiment
Colonel John Quincy Adams Nadenbousch
333 troops present for duty equipped

4th Virginia Infantry Regiment
Major William Terry
257 troops present for duty equipped

5th Virginia Infantry Regiment
Colonel John Henry Stover Funk
345 troops present for duty equipped

27th Virginia Infantry Regiment
Lieutenant-Colonel Daniel McKeloran Shriver
148 troops present for duty equipped

33rd Virginia Infantry Regiment
Captain Jacob Burner Golladay
236 troops present for duty equipped

Battle flag of Major Andrew Brady's 15th Louisiana Infantry Regiment, captured at Spotsylvania in 1864.

close to 25 miles along the Chambersburg Pike to arrive at Gettysburg before darkness fell. Ewell ordered the Division to occupy Culp's Hill if the enemy was not there. In near darkness the Division followed the route of the Gettysburg and York Railroad to the northeast of town. It deployed about a mile northeast of Culp's Hill, just north of the Hanover Road. When scouting parties revealed the hill to be occupied, Johnson did not engage. Pickets were thrown forward and the men slept on their arms.

NICHOLL'S (WILLIAMS') BRIGADE
Colonel Jesse Milton Williams
3 Staff and Field Officers

1st Louisiana Infantry Regiment
Lieutenant-Colonel Michael Nolan
172 troops present for duty equipped

2nd Louisiana Infantry Regiment
Lieutenant-Colonel Ross E. Burke
236 troops present for duty equipped

10th Louisiana Infantry Regiment
Major Thomas N. Powell
226 troops present for duty equipped

14th Louisiana Infantry Regiment
Lieutenant-Colonel David Zable
281 troops present for duty equipped

15th Louisiana Infantry Regiment
Major Andrew Brady
186 troops present for duty equipped

burg on June 5. Entering the Shenandoah Valley, it enjoyed considerable success at the Battle of Winchester during the period June 13-15, capturing some 2,300 Federal prisoners along with eleven colours, at a cost of 14 killed and 74 wounded,

The Division crossed the Potomac on June 18. Responding to orders from Corps Headquarters, on June 29 it began marching eastward toward Gettysburg in order to unite with the balance of the Corps. On July 1 it endured a fatiguing march of

Battle flag of the 48th Virginia Infantry Regiment, also captured later in the war.

JONES' BRIGADE
Brigadier-General John Marshall Jones
7 Staff and Field Officers

21st Virginia Infantry Regiment
Captain William Perkins Moseley
183 troops present for duty equipped

25th Virginia Infantry Regiment
Colonel John Carlton Higginbotham
280 troops present for duty equipped

42nd Virginia Infantry Regiment
Lieutenant-Colonel Robert Woodson Withers
265 troops present for duty equipped

44th Virginia Infantry Regiment
Colonel Norvell Cobb
227 troops present for duty equipped

48th Virginia Infantry Regiment
Lieutenant-Colonel Robert H. Dungan
265 troops present for duty equipped

50th Virginia Infantry Regiment
Lieutenant-Colonel Logan Henry Neal Salyer
240 troops present for duty equipped

Divisional Artillery - Latimer's Battalion of Artillery
Major James W. Latimer
9 Staff and Field Officers

1st Maryland Battery
Captain William F. Dement
(90 troops present for duty equipped)
4 pieces

4th Chesapeake Artillery (Maryland)
Captain William D. Brown
(76 troops present for duty equipped)
4 pieces

Alleghany Artillery (Virginia)
Captain John Cadwalider Carpenter
(91 troops present for duty equipped)
4 pieces

Lynchburg "Lee" Artillery (Virginia)
Captain Charles I. Raine
(90 troops present for duty equipped)
5 pieces

II CSA Army Corps - Rodes' Division

When the mortally-wounded Stonewall Jackson urged a battlefield promotion for Brigadier-General Robert Rodes, he was set on the path to permanent divisional command.

The Division formerly had been led by D.H. Hill. Rodes had commanded a brigade in Hill's Division during the Peninsula Campaign of 1862. In the subsequent reorganisation, Hill's Division, which included Rodes' Brigade, took the basic form that was to continue through the Gettysburg Campaign. In January 1863, Hill departed for North Carolina and Rodes

RODES' DIVISION
Major-General Robert Emmett Rodes
14 Staff and Field Officers

Daniel's Brigade 2,052
Doles' Brigade 1,323
Iverson's Brigade 1,384
Ramseur's Brigade 1,027
Rodes' (O'Neal's) Brigade 1,688
Carter's Artillery Battalion 385

Major-General Robert Emmett Rodes was a graduate of the Virginia Military Institute. He entered service at First Manassas as colonel of the 5th Alabama Infantry. He was one of the army's rising stars.

assumed command by virtue of his seniority.

At Chancellorsville, the Division led the way during Jackson's march. It deployed in the front wave and was the leading unit to strike the Federal flank. As they charged, soldiers heard Rodes' fiery battle cry, "Forward, men, over friend or foe!" It was because of Rodes' inspirational leadership that Jackson recommended Rodes for promotion. Lee obliged and the new

major-general led the Division during the invasion of Pennsylvania. The Division thus had the distinction of being the only one in Lee's army commanded by a non-West Pointer. Rodes had graduated with distinction from the Virginia Military Institute.

Chancellorsville had cost the Division more than 3,000 casualties. In the shuffling of units before the Gettysburg Campaign, the Division lost Colquitt's Georgia Brigade and gained Daniel's North Carolina Brigade.

When the Division began its march north on June 4, it had the satisfaction of knowing it was commanded by an exceptionally gallant officer and one of the army's rising stars.

On June 30 the Division completed a 22-mile march to arrive at Heidlersburg, about nine miles northwest of Gettysburg. The next day, it advanced when, "within 4 miles of the town...the presence of the enemy there in force was announced by the sound of a sharp cannonade, and instant preparations for battle were made."

33

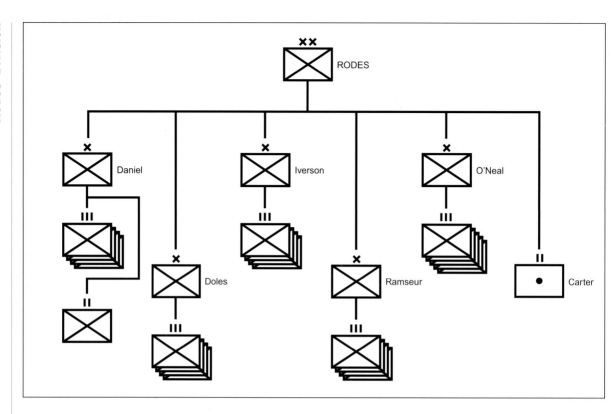

Rodes' Division - Daniel's Brigade

Daniel's Brigade first appeared in the Virginia theatre in April 1862 in time for the Seven Days' Battles. The Brigade barely saw combat during this campaign. The Brigade's losses for the campaign were two killed and 22 wounded. When Lee took the majority of the army away from Richmond for the Second Manassas Campaign, it remained behind to guard Drewry's Bluff on the James river. The Brigade then uneventfully spent the winter of 1862-63 in its home state.

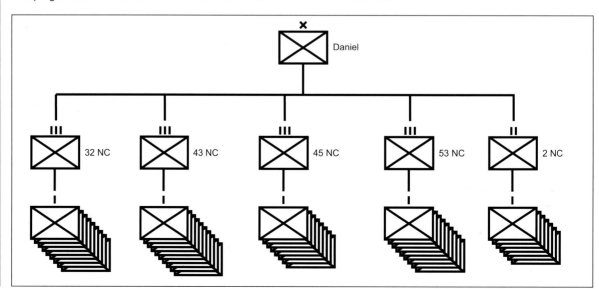

DANIEL'S BRIGADE
Brigadier-General Junius Daniel
4 Staff and Field Officers

Brigadier-General Junius Daniel attended West Point and spent several years as a soldier before retiring to run a family plantation. The 35-year-old North Carolinian had an excellent reputation among his fellow officers.

45th Regiment North Carolina Troops
Lieutenant-Colonel Samuel H. Boyd/
Major John R. Winston
460 troops present for duty equipped

Co. A Rockingham Zollicoffers
Co. B *Name not available*
Co. C Guilford Light Infantrry
Co. E Troublesome Boys
Co. F Dan River Rangers
Co. H Rockingham Guards
Co. I Border Rangers
Co. K North State Boys

When the Brigade entered Carlisle, Pennsylvania, the 32nd enjoyed the honour of unfurling for the first time the new, official battle flag of the Confederate States.

This red flag with a blue cross spangled with white

32nd Regiment North Carolina Troops
Colonel Edmund Crew Brabble
454 troops present for duty equipped

Co. A *Name not available*
Co. B Camden Grays
Co. D *Name not available*
Co. E *Name not available*
Co. F *Name not available*
Co. G *Name not available*
Co. H *Name not available*
Co. I Chatham Rifles
Co. K Franklin Rifles

53rd Regiment North Carolina Troops
Colonel William Allison Owens
322 troops present for duty equipped

Co. A *Name not available*
Co. B *Name not available*
Co. D *Name not available*
Co. E Farmer Boys
Co. F *Name not available*
Co. G Mountain Greys
Co. H Danbury Blues
Co. I *Name not available*
Co. K Wilkes Rangers

The Brigade was one of three Lee summoned from North Carolina to join his army for the invasion. The green 32nd and 53rd North Carolina regiments as well as the inexperienced 2nd North Carolina Battalion were now part of the Brigade. None of these units had ever served with the Army of Northern Virginia.

stars, had been sewn by a group of Richmond ladies and sent to Lee with instructions to give it to a worthy regiment. As an honour to Stonewall Jackson, the flag went down the chain of command into the proud hands of the 32nd. Although the strongest unit in Rodes' Division, the Brigade had very little combat experience.

43rd Regiment North Carolina Troops
Colonel Thomas S. Kenan
572 troops present for duty equipped

Co. A Duplin Rifles
Co. B Union Farmers
Co. C *Name not available*
Co. D *Name not available*
Co. E Edgecombe Boys
Co. F *Name not available*
Co. G Warren Defenders
Co. H Fisher Light Infantry
Co. I Anson Regulators
Co. K Anson Independents

2nd North Carolina Battalion
Lieutenant-Colonel Hezekiah L. Andrews/
Major John M. Hancock/
Captain Van Brown
240 troops present for duty equipped

Co. A Brown Mountain Boys
Co. B *Name not available*
Co. D Cherokee Georgia Mountaineers
Co. E Anthony Grays
Co. F *Name not available*
Co. G *Name not available*
Co. H Madison Guards

Rodes' Division - Doles' Brigade

The four Georgia regiments composing Doles' Brigade began their association on January 19, 1863. On that date the 12th and 21st Georgia

regiments transferred from Hoke's to Doles' Brigade and the 1st and 3rd North Carolina regiments left to join a North Carolina brigade. From this date the Brigade remained intact until the surrender at Appomattox Court House.

The first battle in which the Brigade participated after its consolidation was at Chancellorsville. It was part of

Brigadier-General George Pierce Doles, age 33, had tried unsuccessfully to run away as a teenager to fight in the Mexican War. The Georgia businessman was active in the militia and brought his well-trained company into the war.

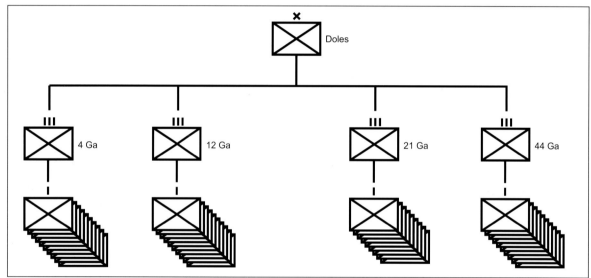

4th Regiment Georgia Volunteer Infantry
Lieutenant-Colonel David Read Evans Winn/
Major Willian Henry Willis
341 troops present for duty equipped

Co. A   Southern Rifles
Co. B   LaGrange Light Guard
Co. C   Twiggs County Volunteers
Co. D   West Point Guard
Co. E   Albany Guard
Co. F   Toombs Volunteers
Co. G   Glover Guards
Co. H   Baldwin Blues
Co. I   Macon County Volunteers
Co. K   Sumter Light Guard

Stonewall Jackson's flank march and deployed in the right centre of Rodes' line. With its left touching the Turnpike, the Brigade swept forward toward the two regiments of Von Gilsa's brigade that faced west. Doles detached two regiments to flank that position. After a brief but fierce fight, these regiments captured the position and two guns. Meanwhile, the remaining two regiments charged forward toward Talley's, defeated two battle lines, and captured five more cannon. The next day the Brigade assaulted the Fairview position and helped carry it after a costly battle.

It had been a triumphant but costly first battle with the Brigade suffering more than 400 casualties. The Brigade was well content with its leader, later calling the former militia officer "one of the bravest, best loved and most accomplished soldiers Georgia furnished to the Confederate army."

It invaded Pennsylvania in high spirits. Having read Northern newspapers claiming the rebellion was near its end, the Brigade responded. Its bands led the march through Chambersburg. With "arms at the right-shoulder shift, the boys stepping out lively to the music, laughing and shouting to the gloomy-faced citizens " the Georgians called out "Here's your played-out rebellion."

On the eve of Gettysburg, the army knew Doles' Brigade to be a hard-hitting unit led by a daring, capable officer. The end of June 30 found the Brigade at the crossroads hamlet of Heidlersburg, nine miles northeast of Gettysburg.

21st Regiment Georgia Volunteer Infantry
Colonel John Thomas Mercer
287 troops present for duty equipped

Co. A Campbell Guards
Co. B Floyd Sharpshooters
Co. C Atlanta Volunteers
Co. D Cedartown Guards
Co. F Ben Hill Infantry
Co. G Dabney Rifles
Co. H Silver Grays
Co. I Stewart Infantry
Co. K Bartow Avengers

12th Regiment Georgia Volunteer Infantry
Colonel Edward Willis
327 troops present for duty equipped

Co. A Mackalee Guards
Co. B Jones County Volunteers
Co. C Davis Rifles
Co. D Calhoun Rifles
Co. E Muscogee Rifles
Co. F Davis Guards
Co. G Putnam Light Infantry
Co. H Central City Blues
Co. I Lowndes County Volunteers
Co. K Marion Guards

44th Regiment Georgia Volunteer Infantry
Colonel Samuel P. Lumpkin/
Major William Hubbard Peebles
364 troops present for duty equipped

Co. A Weems Guards
Co. B Jasper Volunteers
Co. C Johnson Guards
Co. D Estes Guards
Co. E Freeman Volunteers
Co. F Putnam Volunteers
Co. G Huie Guards
Co. H Pike County Volunteers
Co. I Morgan and Henry Volunteers
Co. K Greene County Volunteers

Rodes' Division - Iverson's Brigade

The Brigade, under the command of Brigadier-General Samuel Garland, saw its introduction to combat during the Seven Days' Battles. Here it suffered 844 casualties including a serious wound to Colonel Alfred Iverson, Jr. of the 20th North Carolina.

IVERSON'S BRIGADE
Brigadier-General Alfred Iverson, Jr.
4 Staff and Field Officers

Brigadier-General Alfred Iverson, Jr. aged 34, began his military career in the Mexican War at age 17. His father's friendship with Jefferson Davis may have played a role in his rise to brigade command.

The Brigade was reunited with Iverson at the Battle of South Mountain in September 1862. When Garland went down with a mortal wound, the Brigade routed, losing 187 men missing although Iverson was able to rally the 20th North Carolina late in the day. The colonel temporarily in command at Sharpsburg failed to impress army commander Lee. Consequently, during the army reorganisation in November, Lee promoted Iverson to brigadier-general and brigade command.

The Brigade was not impressed with their leader. Iverson had feuded with his subordinates while colonel of the 20th. Although the Brigade remained in reserve

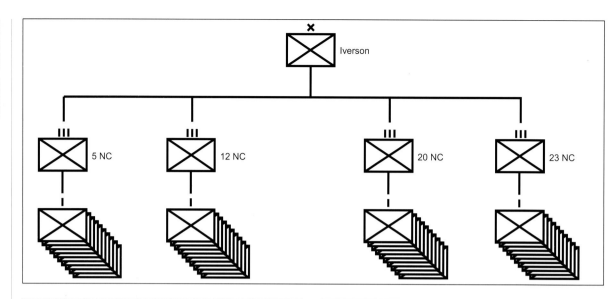

5th North Carolina State Troops
Captain Speight B. West/
Captain Benjamin Robinson
473 troops present for duty equipped

Cos. A thru K. *All Company names not available.*

at Fredericksburg, internal difficulties continued into the winter. On the eve of the Chancellorsville Campaign, Iverson ran foul of Stonewall Jackson. The Brigade was on the far left of the first line during Jackson's flank attack at Chancellorsville. Here it suffered 470 casualties. When Iverson went to the rear on the purported mission of seeking support for his own left flank, many in the Brigade concluded that he was shirking.

Iverson's mediocre performance, vindictive nature, rumours that he had been promoted because of family influence, and hints of cowardice worried the Brigade.

On the eve of the Gettysburg Campaign, relation-

12th Regiment North Carolina Troops
Lieutenant-Colonel William Smith Davis
219 troops present for duty equipped

Co. A Catawba Rifles
Co. B Townsville Guards
Co. C Warren Rifles
Co. D Granville Greys
Co. E Cleveland Guards
Co. F Warren Guards
Co. G Halifax Light Infantry
Co. H Nash Boys
Co. I *Name not available*
Co. K *Name not available*

20th Regiment North Carolina Troops
Lieutenant-Colonel Nelson Slough/
Captain Louis T. Hicks
372 troops present for duty equipped

Co. A Cabarrus Guards
Co. B Cabarrus Black Boys
Co. C Columbus Guards No.3
Co. D Columbus Guards No.4
Co. E Confederate Grays
Co. F Holmes Riflemen
Co. G Brunswick Guards
Co. H Independent Blues
Co. I Sampson Greys
Co. K Columbus Guards No.2

ships among Brigade officers and Iverson remained poor. Rife with rancour, the Brigade's future promised trouble.

23rd Regiment North Carolina Troops
Colonel Daniel Harvey Christie/
Lieutenant-Colonel R.D. Johnston/
Major Charles Christopher Blacknall/
Captain William H. Johnston
316 troops present for duty equipped

Co. A Anson Ellis Rifles
Co. B Hog Hill Guards
Co. C Montgomery Volunteers
Co. D Pee Dee Guards
Co. E Granville Plough Boys
Co. F Catawba Guards
Co. G Granville Rifles
Co. H Gaston Guards
Co. I Granville Stars
Co. K Beattie's Ford Riflemen

Rodes' Division - Ramseur's Brigade

The North Carolina regiments who composed the brigade that would march to Gettysburg, entered Virginia in 1862 in time to participate at the Seven Days' Battles. It charged up the slope of Malvern Hill on July 1. Among its 863 casualties was the Colonel of the 49th North Carolina, Stephen Dodson Ramseur.

As part of Major-General D.H. Hill's Division, the Brigade participated in the invasion of Maryland. When it lost its commander, Brigadier-General George B. Anderson, at the Battle of Sharpsburg, army commander Lee summoned Ramseur back from his convalescence to replace him. Lee had been impressed by Ramseur's bravery at Malvern Hill and his ability to

> ### RAMSEUR'S BRIGADE
> ### *Brigadier-General Stephen Dodson Ramseur*
> ### 4 Staff and Field Officers

under the command of Colonel Bryan Grimes, the Brigade was not heavily engaged during the Battle of Fredericksburg, losing eight killed and 51 wounded.

The Brigade received its new commander, Ramseur, in January 1863. Although his arm was still in a sling, his martial bearing, amiability, and enthusiasm quickly won over his men. They demonstrated their faith at the Battle of Chancellorsville. The Brigade deployed in the front-line of Jackson's flank attack on May 2 and

Brigadier-General Steven Dodson Ramseur had a creditable performance at West Point, graduating just before the war broke out. A natural fighter "his whole being seemed to kindle and glow amid the excitement of danger."

> ### 2nd North Carolina
> ### State Troops
> ### *Major Daniel W. Hurttl*
> ### *Captain James Turner Scales*
> ### 243 troops present for duty equipped
>
> Co. A *Name not available*
> Co. B *Name not available*
> Co. C Rip Van Winkles
> Co. D *Name not available*
> Co. E Guilford Guards
> Co. F *Name not available*
> Co. G Jones Rifle Guards
> Co. H *Name not available*
> Co. I Beaufort Rifles
> Co. K Elm City Cadets

train and discipline his commands. Promoted to brigadier-general at age 25, Ramseur was the youngest general in the Confederate army. Meanwhile,

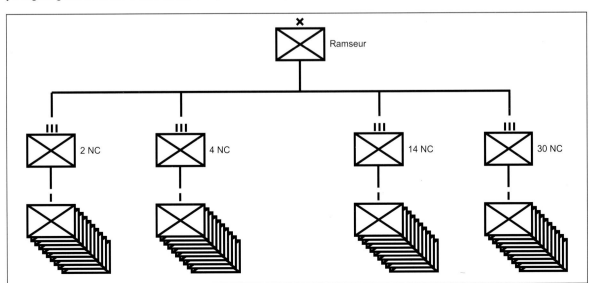

helped crush the Federal XI Corps. On May 3, the Brigade continued its advance with Ramseur at its head literally striding over the bodies of prostrate, disheartened soldiers. Charging into intense fire, the Brigade overran a defended breastwork. Isolated and exposed, it fought until nearly out of ammunition.

Eventually the Stonewall Brigade rallied to come to its support. The Brigade suffered the heaviest losses of any Confederate brigade in the battle; 151 killed, 529 wounded, and 108 missing.

The skill with which Ramseur handled them impressed superiors and the Brigade alike. Four veteran regiments led by a tactically adroit commander promised a fine future.

14th Regiment North Carolina Troops
Colonel Risden Tyler Bennett
306 troops present for duty equipped

Co. A Roanoke Minute Men
Co. B *Name not available*
Co. C Anson Guard
Co. D Cleveland Blues
Co. E Oak City Guards
Co. F Rough-and-Ready Guard
Co. G *Name not available*
Co. H Stanly Marksmen
Co. I Davidson Wild Cats
Co. K *Name not available*

4th North Carolina State Troops
Colonel Bryan Grimes
196 troops present for duty equipped

Co. A *Name not available*
Co. B *Name not available*
Co. C *Name not available*
Co. D Goldsboro Volunteers
Co. E Southern Guards
Co. F Wilson Light Infantry
Co. G Davie Sweep Stakes
Co. H *Name not available*
Co. I Pamlico Rifles
Co. K *Name not available*

30th Regiment North Carolina Troops
Colonel Francis Marion Parker/ Major William Walter Sillers
278 troops present for duty equipped

Co. A Sampson Rangers
Co. B Nat Macon Guards
Co. C Brunswick Double Quicks
Co. D *Name not available*
Co. E Duplin Turpentine Boys
Co. F Sparta Band
Co. G Granville Rangers
Co. H *Name not available*
Co. I *Name not available*
Co. K *Name not available*

Rodes' Division - Rodes' (O'Neal's) Brigade

The five veteran Alabama regiments composing Colonel Edward O'Neal's Brigade had been organised together early in the war. The 3rd, 5th and 6th Regiments formed in Alabama's capital in late spring and summer of 1861. The 12th mustered in Richmond in July 1861, while the 26th Regiment formed in Richmond in March 1862, through the expansion of the 3rd Battalion.

The battle history of these fine Alabama units is virtually the history of the Confederate army in Virginia. The 5th and 6th Regiments, the latter under the command of then Colonel Robert Rodes, were present at First Manassas but were not engaged. When Rodes ascended to brigade command, Colonel John B. Gordon, the officer who would command a brigade himself at Gettysburg, succeeded him. The 12th Regiment joined the brigade in time for the Peninsula Campaign in the spring of 1862. As part of Major-

RODES' (O'NEAL'S) BRIGADE
Colonel Edward Asbury O'Neal
3 Staff and Field Officers

General Daniel Hill's Division, Rodes' Brigade saw limited action at the Battle of Williamsburg. Here the 26th Regiment, which was also in Hill's Division, served in Brigadier-General Gabriel Rains' Brigade. Colonel O'Neal commanded this regiment.

O'Neal was a native of northern Alabama. He was a lawyer who made an unsuccessful bid for a congressional seat in 1848. Thereafter, he became one of the state's leading secessionist politicians. When Alabama left the Union, O'Neal joined the "Calhoun Guards" as a captain. Although he had no military experience, he had become colonel by the time the 26th fought in the

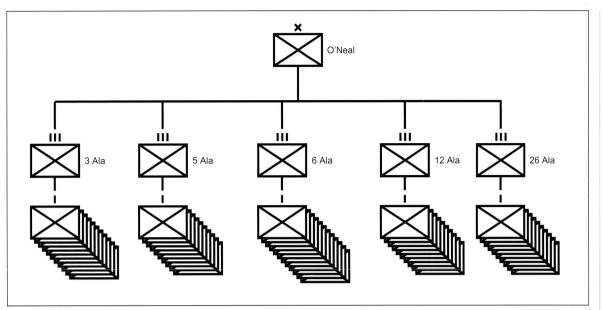

Colonel Edward Asbury O'Neal was an Alabama lawyer and politician with no previous military experience. Although the 45-year-old was brave, a series of command blunders cost him promotion to general.

Peninsula Campaign.

All four regiments participated in the bloody fighting at Seven Pines. Among the 1,099 casualties suffered in Rodes' Brigade was the colonel of the 12th who died in combat. The 6th Regiment suffered 59% losses at this battle. Rains' Brigade also experienced heavy combat.

Colonel O'Neal distinguished himself during the Brigade's charge by exhibiting reckless disregard for his own safety. He received a wound from a shell fragment but recovered in time for the Seven Days' Battles.

Colonel Cullen Andrews Battle (here as Brigadier-General) commanded the 3rd Alabama Infantry Regiment at Gettysburg.

3rd Alabama Infantry Regiment
Colonel Cullen Andrews Battle
350 troops present for duty equipped

Co. A Mobile Cadets
Co. B Gulf City Guards
Co. C Tuskegee Light Infantry
Co. D Southern Rifles
Co. E Washington Light Infantry
Co. F Metropolitan Guards
Co. G Montgomery True Blues
Co. H Lowndes Beauregards
Co. I Wetumpka Light Guards
Co. K Mobile Rifles
Co. L Dixie Eagles

The five regiments that were to serve at Gettysburg organised into Rodes' Brigade before the Seven Days' Battles. Here again they witnessed stern fighting. During the course of the campaign the Brigade lost 112

5th Alabama Infantry Regiment
Colonel Josephus Marion Hall
317 troops present for duty equipped

Co. A *Name not available*
Co. B *Name not available*
Co. C *Name not available*
Co. D Monroe Guards
Co. E *Name not available*
Co. F Cahaba Rifles
Co. G *Name not available*
Co. H Warrior Guards
Co. I *Name not available*
Co. K *Name not available*

6th Alabama Infantry Regiment
Colonel James Newell Lightfoot/
Major Isaac Franklin Culver/
Captain Milledge L. Bowie
382 troops present for duty equipped

Co. A Henry Grays
Co. B *Name not available*
Co. C *Name not available*
Co. D Raccoon Roughs
Co. E *Name not available*
Co. F Russell Volunteers
Co. G *Name not available*
Co. H *Name not available*
Co. I *Name not available*
Co. K Columbia Blues
Co. L Autauga Rifles
Co. M *Name not available*

brigade command stepped the senior colonel, O'Neal. This displeased Rodes. However, unless there were compelling reasons, Robert E. Lee adhered to the dictates of seniority and state association.

The Brigade followed Colonel O'Neal into combat during the Chancellorsville Campaign. After participating in "Stonewall" Jackson's famous flank march on May 2, the Brigade deployed. The dense underbrush made deployment time consuming. As part of the Division's advance, the Alabama Brigade began to move forward. O'Neal had forgotten to order his skirmishers to advance ahead of his brigade. When the Brigade overtook the skirmish line, it halted, throwing the entire advance into a snarl. Rodes personally intervened to get the advance rolling again. Although the attack proved successful in crushing the Federal flank, O'Neal's command muddle had not escaped notice.

During the Chancellorsville Campaign, the Brigade lost 90 killed, 538 wounded, and 188 missing. Among the wounded was O'Neal, who was hit for the third time. No one questioned O'Neal's bravery. However his competence for brigade command was suspect. In his after-action report, Rodes complained about the "orders not having been promptly given" to the Brigade's skirmishers.

In the post-Chancellorsville reorganisation, Lee intended that O'Neal become the permanent leader of the Alabama Brigade and recommended him for promotion to brigadier-general. Although former brigade and now divisional commander Rodes was personally cordial with O'Neal, he had recommended a different officer. The authorities in Richmond approved Lee's recommendation and issued his commission on June 6. Curiously, the army commander did not follow through. Instead, he kept the commission a secret for the time being.

Clearly, he was having doubts about O'Neal's capacity for command. His performance at Gettysburg would determine if he deserved brigade command.

killed and 458 wounded, including a mortal wound to the colonel of the 5th Alabama. Rodes cited Colonel O'Neal's bravery at Gaines' Mill while acting brigade commander, John Gordon, commended his "gallant conduct" at Malvern Hill. The Brigade had forged a valiant reputation at high cost.

After avoiding the fighting at Second Manassas, Rodes' Brigade participated in the invasion of Maryland in September 1862. At the Battle of South Mountain, it lost 422 men including a serious thigh wound to Colonel O'Neal and a wound to Lieutenant-Colonel James Lightfoot, the officer who was to command the 6th Alabama at Gettysburg. At Sharpsburg it suffered another 203 casualties.

While O'Neal convalesced back home in Alabama, the Brigade saw only light action at Fredericksburg. Then, in January 1863, it experienced a command change. At that time divisional commander D.H. Hill transferred to North Carolina. Major-General Robert Rodes replaced Hill. Into the resultant vacancy for

12th Alabama Infantry Regiment
Colonel Samuel Bonneau Pickins
317 troops present for duty equipped

Co. A Guard Lafayette
Co. B Coosa Independents
Co. C Independent Rifles
Co. D Coffee Rangers
Co. E *Name not available*
Co. F Macon Confederates
Co. G Paint Rock River Sharpshooters
Co. H Magnolia Rifles
Co. I Southern Foresters
Co. K Tom Watts' Rebels

26th Alabama Infantry Regiment
Lieutenant-Colonel John Chapman Goodgame
319 troops present for duty equipped

Co. A *Name not available*
Co. B *Name not available*
Co. C *Name not available*
Co. D *Name not available*
Co. E *Name not available*
Co. F *Name not available*
Co. G *Name not available*
Co. H Sons of '76
Co. I *Name not available*
Co. K *Name not available*

Rodes' Division - Carter's Artillery Battalion

Carter's Battalion came into formal existence after Brigadier-General Pendleton submitted his plan to reorganise the army's artillery on February 11, 1863. Pendleton wrote, "that in each corps the artillery be arranged into battalions, to consist for the most part of four batteries each, a particu-

---

Divisional Artillery
Lieutenant-Colonel Thomas Henry Carter
9 Staff and Field Officers

---

lar battalion ordinarily to attend to a certain division." Pendleton recommended Carter for leadership because of his "distinguished services, and eminent merit."

The Battalion, with eighteen guns, actively supported Rodes' Division during the fighting at Chancellorsville. On May 2, it trailed the infantry during Jackson's flank march and occupied a position around Wilderness Tavern when Rodes' infantry attacks began. When the Battalion tried to advance, Federal artillery fire struck it while it was in road column and caused the horses to become unmanageable. The Battalion had to retire to refit. On May 3, it bombarded the Federal position at

The 10-pounder Parrott gun, in ideal conditions, using 1-pound of powder could fire a 10fi-pound case shot round out to 930 yards.

Fairview and then rapidly displaced forward to occupy the commanding heights. When the Union troops tried to make a stand near the Chancellor House, the Battalion delivered telling enfilade fire. The endemic

---

Carter's Battalion of Artillery

Jefferson Davis Artillery (Alabama)
Captain William J. Reese
(79 troops present for duty equipped)
4 3-inch rifled guns

King William Artillery (Virginia)
Captain William Pleasants Page Carter
(103 troops present for duty equipped)
2 10-pounder Parrott rifled guns
2 12-pounder Napoleon guns

Morris Artillery (Virginia)
Captain Richard Channing Moore Page/
Lieutenant Samuel H. Pendleton
(114 troops present for duty equipped)
4 12-pounder Napoleon guns

Orange Artillery (Virginia)
Captain Charles William Fry
(80 troops present for duty equipped)
2 3-inch rifled guns
2 10-pounder Parrott rifled guns

---

problem for Confederate gunners, the unreliability of the fuses for the shells, impaired the artillery's effectiveness. A large percentage of shells failed to burst while others exploded prematurely. This made ranging near guesswork. Veteran artillery officers recalled that they could fire twelve rounds but because of the erratic shell bursts they would still not know the correct range. Nonetheless, the Battalion contributed valuable fire support at Chancellorsville. It suffered nine killed and 37 wounded during the campaign.

The Battalion was a thoroughly experienced organisation. The Jeff Davis Artillery and Orange Light Artillery had formed in May 1861; the King William Artillery in June; and the Morris Artillery two months later in August 1861.

BATTALION EQUIPMENT

16 Caissons
236 Horses
2 Forges

II CSA Corps Reserve Artillery

When Lee authorised a reorganisation of the army's artillery, the objective was to improve efficiency while equalising artillery support among all of the infantry. Chief of Artillery Pendleton hoped this could be accomplished with "the least possible disturbance to existing relationships." Infantry and artillery officers alike wanted to preserve familiar associations.

Accordingly, Dance's Battalion, which had been a fix-

II ARMY CORPS RESERVE ARTILLERY
Colonel John Thompson Brown
4 Staff and Field Officers

ture in II Corps Reserve Artillery, remained. Its sister unit, McIntosh's Battalion, transferred to III Corps Reserve. Replacing McIntosh's was Nelson's Battalion, which as recently as the Chancellorsville Campaign had been part of the now disbanded general army reserve. Pendleton described Nelson as a "gallant and efficient" officer. Colonel John T. Brown remained in command of II Corps Reserve Artillery.

After entering the Shenandoah Valley, Dance's Battalion participated in the combats around Winchester. Its fire support assisted the infantry to capture four 20-pounder Parrott rifles along with seventeen 3-inch rifles. The Confederate gunners in the

Nelson's Battalion of Artillery
Lieutenant-Colonel William Nelson
9 Staff and Field Officers

Amherst Artillery (Virginia)
Captain Thomas Jellis Kirkpartick
(105 troops present for duty equipped)
4 pieces

Fluvanna Artillery (Virginia)
Captain John Livingston Massie
(90 troops present for duty equipped)
4 pieces

Georgia Regular Battery
Captain John Milledge, Jr.
(73 troops present for duty equipped)
3 pieces

RESERVE ARTILLERY EQUIPMENT

33 Caissons
492 Horses
9 Forges
1 Battery Wagon

Corps Reserve exchanged their worn pieces for this superior Federal ordnance with the Rockbridge Artillery acquiring two 20-pounder Parrotts.

On the night of June 30, the Artillery Reserve was between Green Village and Scotland. They were trailing Johnson's Division a little north and west of Chambersburg. It was not until late on July 1 that the two battalions of the II Corps Reserve Artillery arrived at Gettysburg in time to participate in the fighting on the next day.

1st Virginia Artillery Battalion
Captain Willis Jefferson Dance
9 Staff and Field Officers

2nd Company, Richmond Howitzers (Virginia)
Captain David Watson
(64 troops present for duty equipped)
4 pieces

3rd Company, Richmond Howitzers (Virginia)
Captain Benjamin Hodges Smith, Jr.
(62 troops present for duty equipped)
4 pieces

1st Rockbridge Artillery (Virginia)
Captain Archibald Graham
(85 troops present for duty equipped)
4 pieces

Powhatan Artillery (Virginia)
Lieutenant John M. Cunningham
(78 troops present for duty equipped)
4 pieces

Salem Flying Artillery (Virginia)
Lieutenant Charles Beale Griffin
(69 troops present for duty equipped)
4 pieces

II CORPS BATTLES

July 1 - 1400 - 1500 hrs

Hasty Assault

Rodes' Division approached Gettysburg from the north. Four miles from the town it entered within earshot of III Corps' battle along McPherson's Ridge. Recognising that the Division was on the flank of the Federal forces opposing III Corps, Rodes resolved to make a covered approach and deliver a flank attack. The Division marched through the woods on Oak Hill undetected. It then deployed on a three- brigade-front from left to right - Doles, O'Neal, Iverson. Two batteries from Carter's Artillery Battalion unlimbered along the crest of Oak Hill where their eight guns enjoyed a commanding field of fire. The deployment was complete by 1330 hours, by which time Rodes could see elements of the Federal XI Corps moving north from Gettysburg to oppose his left flank.

From Oak Hill the King William Artillery and the Orange Artillery punished the Union infantry with enfilade fire. However, it brought down severe counter-battery fire that in a short period of time cost the former four killed and seven wounded.

Meanwhile, the Battalion's other two batteries moved to the Division's left to oppose the infantry emerging from Gettysburg. Rodes also assigned Doles' Brigade the duty of containing these Federal troops. He ordered O'Neal to advance southward along the eastern slopes of Oak Ridge while Iverson's Brigade matched O'Neal by moving along the crest. Daniel's Brigade was to advance en echelon behind Iverson's right while Ramseur's Brigade remained in close reserve. The target of this manoeuvre was the open Federal flank that could be seen in the fields just north of the unfinished railroad.

Here danger lay hidden. In his zeal to take advantage of a perceived opportunity, Rodes and his brigadiers neglected adequate reconnaissance. Consequently, O'Neal and Iverson encountered unsuspected, ferocious resistance along Oak Ridge itself.

Before beginning the charge, O'Neal's Brigade had retired a short distance into the woods to avoid Federal artillery fire. Rodes had personally positioned the 3rd Alabama on the Brigade's right. Then, as O'Neal was aligning his regiments for the advance, Rodes pulled the 5th Alabama out of his Brigade line and moved it eastward to cover the gap between O'Neal and Doles.

With his limited experience with brigade command, O'Neal concluded that he no longer controlled these two regiments. Consequently, at about 1415 hours he advanced with only three regiments. In spite of careful orders from Rodes, O'Neal misdirected their line of advance. When the Alabama regiments advanced to within 200 yards of the enemy, the Federal soldiers belonging to Baxter's Brigade opened fire. A waiting defender describes the scene: "Their line of battle,

0800 hrs	0900	1000	1100	1200	1300	1400	1500	1600	1700	1800
	pages 81-84						85-87	88-89		

45

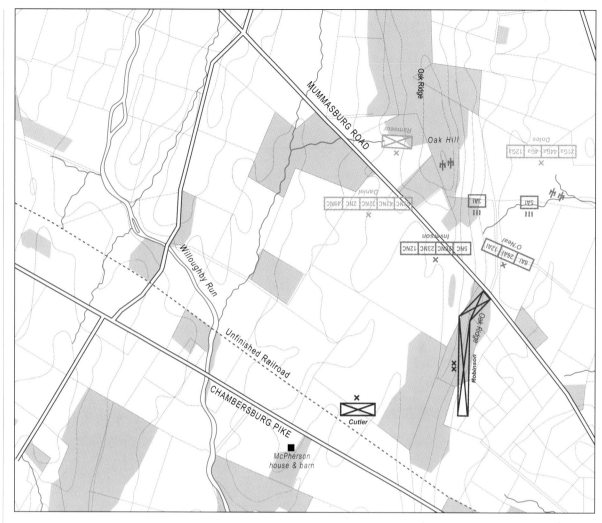

Map labels: MUMMASBURG ROAD, Oak Ridge, Oak Hill, Ramseur, Doles, 21GA 44GA 4GA 12GA, Daniel, 53NC 43NC 32NC 2NC 45NC, 3AL, 5AL, Iverson, O'Neal, 5NC 20NC 23NC 12NC, 6AL 26AL 12AL, Willoughby Run, Robinson, Oak Ridge, Unfinished Railroad, CHAMBERSBURG PIKE, Cutler, McPherson house & barn

covered by a cloud of busy skirmishers, came driving through the wood...Waiting until they were in easy range, the order was given, 'Commence firing.' With the sharp crack of the muskets a fleecy cloud of smoke rolled down the front of the brigade and the Minie balls zipped and buzzed with a merry chorus toward the Southern line, which halted, and after a brief contest, retired to the shelter of the woods."

While the three regiments melted before the severe frontal fire, the 45th New York, belonging to Schimmelfennig's Brigade, took advantage of O'Neal's exposed left flank to perform a wheel and then deliver enfilade fire. Union artillery also battered this exposed flank. Meanwhile, O'Neal, who had displayed courage on other fields and been wounded three times, hung back with the 5th Alabama. Here, to

Approx. 1415 hours - As Rodes' Division moves south along Oak Ridge, O'Neal's Brigade springs the trap. It is rapidly repulsed. Robinson's Federal Division then engages Iverson's left flank and draws the Confederates into a protracted firefight.

his disgust, Rodes found him. Furthermore, as if to avoid exposure, O'Neal had sent the horses belonging to him and his staff to the rear. This made it difficult to render effective brigade leadership. Rodes ordered the 5th to charge to support the beleaguered three regiments. Simultaneously, the Morris Artillery delivered close-range supporting fire. During this phase of the combat, the Morris Artillery suffered most of its extremely heavy losses that totalled 4 killed, 26 wounded, and 17 horses out of action.

0800 hrs	0900	1000	1100	1200	1300	1400	1500	1600	1700	1800
	pages 81-84						85-87	88-89		

The charge of the 5th Alabama could not retrieve the situation. According to Colonel Pickens' report, his 12th Alabama had "suffered severely in this attack. It was impossible for us to hold the position we had gained any longer without being cut to pieces or compelled to surrender." After a combat that may have lasted for only fifteen minutes, the attacking regiments retired in disorder about 300 yards before reforming.

The Brigade's commander had not shown well in this engagement. O'Neal had virtually lost control of the brigade and by so doing committed them to a premature, and useless slaughter.During their abortive charge the losses in killed and wounded were: 6th Alabama, 131; 12th Alabama, 83; 26th Alabama, 130.

The brevity of their charge left Iverson's Brigade virtually alone as it advanced along the slopes of Oak Ridge. Iverson had understood that he was to coordinate his advance with O'Neal. When he sent an officer to watch for O'Neal's advance, that officer returned almost immediately with the unwelcome news that O'Neal was already under way. Consequently, by the time Iverson's four North Carolina regiments began their advance at about 1430 hours, O'Neal's Brigade had already been repulsed. This would allow the defenders belonging to Baxter's Brigade to turn the full weight of their fire against Iverson alone.

The Brigade marched south through a timothy grass field that was devoid of cover. The men carried shouldered muskets and proceeded "as evenly as if on parade." There were no skirmishers leading the way. The soldiers had no idea that hidden behind a stone wall, a Federal line stretched at right angle to their line of advance. Having suffered heavily at Chancellorsville, the Brigade was short of officers. Worse still, Iverson, like O'Neal, did not join them but instead remained behind at the start line.

At ranges of about 100 yards, the hidden Federals opened fire. A sheet of flame and smoke rose from the wall as hundreds of bullets poured into the North Carolinians' flank. The shocking fire stopped the Brigade in its tracks. Although men "were falling like leaves in a storm," they attempted to make a stand and return the fire. It proved futile. An officer in the 20th North Carolina wrote, "I believe every man who stood up was either killed or wounded." Leaderless, small knots of men huddled in a shallow swale about 80 yards from the stone wall and here they were slaughtered. A few hours later a rebel gunner passed through the field and counted 79 North Carolina soldiers dead

on the ground, arrayed in a perfectly dressed line. Iverson's fallen would later be buried here and the local population would retain a dread fear of venturing near the ground they called 'Iverson's Pits.'

The men's courage now cost them dearly: "Unable to advance, unwilling to retreat, the brigade lay in this hollow or depression in the field and fought as best it could." So feeble was their resistance, that when the Federal troops scampered over the wall and rushed through the swale, they easily collected about 300 prisoners. Meanwhile, well to the rear, Iverson witnessed his men's ordeal. Possibly because he was drunk, or perhaps because he was badly unnerved, Iverson reported to Rodes that one of his regiments had raised a surrender flag and gone over to the enemy!

Only the 12th North Carolina, by virtue of being farthest away from the wall, escaped the terrible carnage. Suffering 56 casualties, it lost fewer than half as many men as the other three regiments. A surviving officer spoke for the balance of the brigade when he opened his account of the history of the 20th North Carolina with the words, "Initiated at Seven Pines, sacrificed at Gettysburg, surrendered at Appomattox." Most of the Brigade's losses occurred during this phase of the fighting. They totalled 12 officers and 118 men killed, 33 officers and 349 men wounded, and 20 officers and 288 men missing. This grim total represented 60% of the Brigade's strength.

A survivor of Iverson's blunder later wrote, "Deep and long must the desolate homes and orphan children of North Carolina rue the rashness of that hour." The dying Colonel Christie of the 23rd North Carolina had his men gathered about him and pledged that they would never again have "the Imbecile Iverson" command them in battle.

General Rodes had perceived a Chancellorsville-like opportunity to crush an exposed Federal flank. Because he had been in a hurry to capitalise, he was forced to lead the charge with his two least experienced brigades. Worse, he had not properly scouted his line of advance. O'Neal and Iverson, in turn, had failed to position skirmishers in front of their advancing lines and then failed to accompany their men into battle. The hasty assault along Oak Ridge was a staggering debut for the entire Division. Because of his failure at brigade leadership on July 1, Robert E. Lee would return O'Neal's commission as brigadier-general to Richmond. He never advanced beyond colonel.

0800 hrs	0900	1000	1100	1200	1300	1400	1500	1600	1700	1800
	pages 81-84						85-87	88-89		

II CORPS BATTLES
July 1 1500 - 1700 hrs

Daniel Carries the Field

When divisional commander Major-General Rodes conceived his assault against the right flank of the Federal I Corps, he stationed the Division's largest element, Daniel's Brigade, 200 yards behind the right-rear of Iverson's Brigade. Daniel's orders were to give close-support to Iverson's advance.

After Iverson engaged Baxter's Brigade along the slopes of Oak Ridge, Daniel received a request for assistance. He sent the 32nd, 43rd, and 53rd Regiments. Meanwhile, the 2nd Battalion and the 45th Regiment continued southeast toward the unfinished railroad cut. These latter units made an oblique attack against Union troops belonging to Stone's Brigade. Seeing the North Carolinians advance, Stone sent the 149th New York to occupy the railroad cut.

When the 45th North Carolina began climbing a fence within pistol range of the cut, the New Yorkers delivered a deadly volley. Federal artillery from the area around McPherson's barn contributed a telling fire. Still the 45th pressed forward to within 30 yards of the cut.

Here another volley battered it, followed by a bayonet charge from the 149th New York. The rebels fell back before this charge and reformed under heavy fire. According to a veteran captain, here "the regiment suffered more than it ever did in the same length of time." Among the casualties was Lieutenant-Colonel Boyd.

Rallying his men, General Daniel attacked again with his entire brigade. Once more the 45th Regiment and 2nd Battalion bore the brunt of the defenders' fire. The intense Federal musketry and artillery fire stopped the charge at the fenceline. A musketry duel ensued at a range of about 30 yards, but the advantage lay with the defenders who were sheltered by the railroad cut and by the stone barn south of the cut.

Having suffered two repulses, Daniel carefully prepared his third attempt. In his own words, he ordered the 32nd North Carolina "to move forward on the right, and get a position where they could reach the flank of the enemy, posted about the barn and in the woods in the rear of the barn." By this manoeuvre, the 32nd would be linked with Pender's Division. However, unbeknownst to Daniel, the Federal line had already begun to waver in the face of Pender's aggressive frontal attack.

The 32nd managed to cross Chambersburg Pike west of the cut. Resting his left flank on the cut, Colonel Brabble led the Regiment in a charge toward the McPherson Barn. The Regiment seemed to be unsupported. Amid a "terrific fire", it reached the vicinity of the barn but receiving hostile fire on three sides, it retired to its start line.

The problem was that the balance of the Brigade

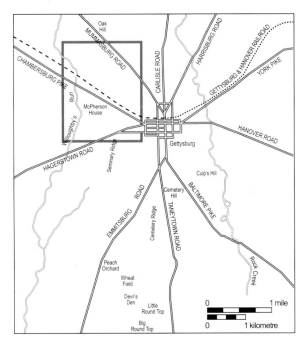

0800 hrs	0900	1000	1100	1200	1300	1400	1500	1600	1700	1800
	pages 81-84						85-87	88-89		

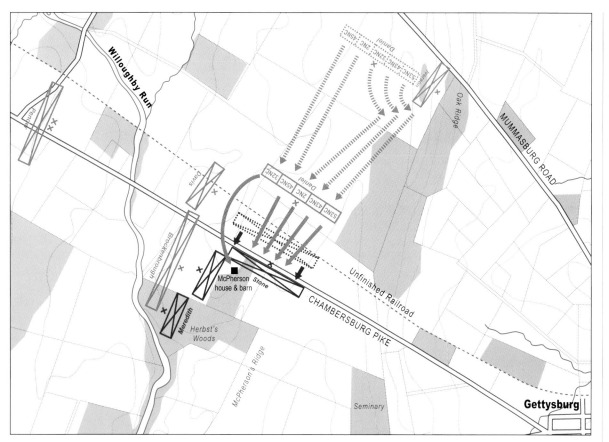

could not charge straight across the cut itself but instead had to manoeuvre around it while under close-range fire.

When Colonel Brabble saw that the other regiments had managed to change front to pass around the obstruction, he led his men forward again. This time their charge helped dislodge the Federal artillery that had been the backbone of the Union defence along the railroad cut.

Meanwhile, "The 45th Regiment and 2nd Battalion, gallantly led by their commanders and supported by the rest of the line, advanced at a charge, driving the enemy from the cut in confusion, killing and wounding many and taking some prisoners; also compelling their artillery to retire from the barn."

Following this success, Daniel reoriented his units in order to advance toward Oak Ridge. Assisted by Iverson's 12th North Carolina, the only regiment of that brigade that had not suffered severely during Iverson's initial assault, the Brigade helped carry the heights "with very heavy loss." Here the 45th North Carolina

Approx. 1515 hours - With the three regiments, which had been detached to help Iverson on Oak Ridge returned, Daniel's Brigade makes two assaults on the Railroad cut before outflanking Stone's Federals and taking the position.

captured some 188 prisoners and recaptured the flag that Iverson's 20th North Carolina had lost earlier.

Daniel's Brigade pursued to the outskirts of Gettysburg, scooping up groups of prisoners by the handful. Here it received orders to halt and return to the railroad cut. Its fighting on the first day at Gettysburg was over.

That combat had cost the Brigade some 750 men, about 37% of its strength. The 2nd Battalion, and 32nd and 45th Regiments had borne the brunt of the action. In his official report, General Rodes commended the Brigade:

"The conduct of General Daniel and his brigade in this most desperate engagement elicited the admiration and praise of all who witnessed it."

0800 hrs	0900	1000	1100	1200	1300	1400	1500	1600	1700	1800
	pages 81-84						85-87	88-89		

II CORPS BATTLES
July 1 1500 - 1700 hrs

Early Intervenes

About noon, when Rodes' Division reached the field, Rodes assigned Doles' Brigade of crack Georgia infantry the task of securing his Division's left flank until Early's Division arrived. About 40 minutes later, when Major-General Howard committed two divisions onto the plain north of Gettysburg, Doles was in trouble.

From the eastern slope of Oak Hill, the Morris Artillery engaged the Union guns deploying north of Gettysburg. A duel at 500 yards range ensued, during which the Morris Artillery suffered heavily, losing 30 men and 17 horses. The Jeff Davis and the King William Artillery shifted front to join their sister battery and re-establish fire superiority. It was an advantage the Confederates were not to relinquish again.

By 1400 hours the two Union divisions completed their deployment north of Gettysburg and advanced against Doles. The yankees drove back Doles' skirmishers who had occupied Blocher's Knoll. Outnumbered, and in danger of envelopment, Doles skilfully fended off disaster until the help he needed dramatically arrived.

The mid-morning of July 1 found Major-General Jubal Early's Division near Heidlersburg. Here Early received a note from Lieutenant-General Ewell to march toward Gettysburg. Shortly before 1500 hours, Early arrived within sight of Gettysburg. He saw Rodes' Division engaged with Federal forces. He also saw that those enemy forces had left their right flank dangling in the air. Moreover, by good fortune Early's men were perfectly positioned to take advantage.

Early deployed three of his brigades to attack Howard's XI Corps. Extending west of the Harrisburg Road was Gordon's Brigade minus the 26th Georgia which was detached to support Jones' divisional artillery battalion. East of the road were Hays' and Avery's Brigades. Well to the rear, also east of the

Harrisburg Road was Smith's Brigade. Between Smith and the front-line troops was Jones' Artillery Battalion.

At 1530 hours the Division's assault began. Until this time all across the field, Federal units had repulsed Confederate attacks. Early's intervention was about to change the tide of battle. The plan, according to Early was simple: "Gordon's brigade was then ordered forward to the support of Doles' brigade, which was on Rodes' left, and was being pressed by a considerable force...which had advanced...to a wooded hill [Blocher's Knoll] on the west side of Rock Creek...and as soon as Gordon was fairly engaged with this force, Hays' and Hoke's [Avery's] brigades were ordered forward in line, and the artillery, supported by Smith's brigade, was ordered to follow."

The initial target of Gordon's advance were the Union

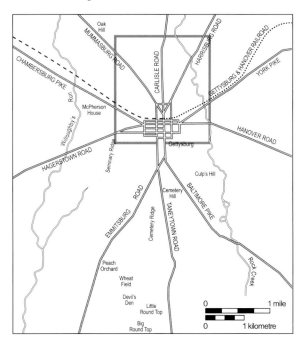

0800 hrs	0900	1000	1100	1200	1300	1400	1500	1600	1700	1800
	pages 81-84						85-87	88-89		

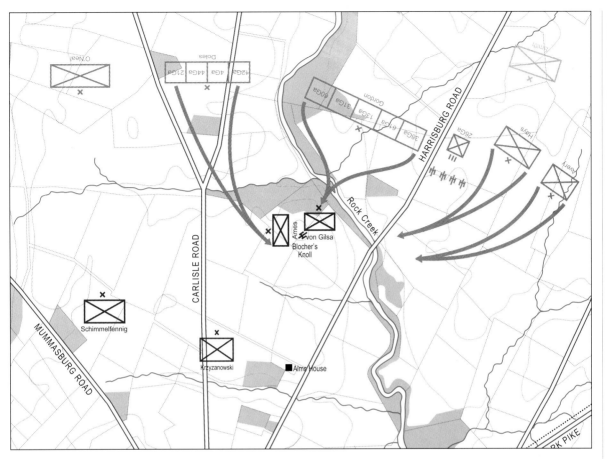

troops on Blocher's Knoll. Twelve guns belonging to the Louisiana Guard Artillery and the two Virginia batteries, the Courtney Artillery and the Staunton Artillery, prepared the way. Their close-range fire into the flank of Barlow's massed infantry disrupted the defenders. A staff officer later recalled that he had never seen guns "better served than Jones' were on this occasion."

Moreover, some rebel gunners fired at a Union battery on the knoll with great effect. That battery's return fire killed two and wounded five Louisiana gunners. One Union round struck the muzzle of a Louisiana 12-pounder Napoleon, knocking it out of action. Three other pieces were disabled by faulty ammunition.

In addition to valuable artillery support, Early's men benefited from the exertions of Doles' Brigade. In his after-action report Doles described his tactical response to the aggressive advance by elements of the Federal XI Corps: the Brigade "moved by the left flank, to meet any attack the enemy might attempt on our left and rear. We found the enemy strongly posted,

1530 hours - Early's Division co-operates with Doles' Brigade from Rodes' Division to drive the Union troops from Blocher's Knoll.

with infantry and artillery, on the hill [Blocher's Knoll] from which our skirmishers had been driven. The brigade of General Gordon...having made a conjunction with our left, we moved forward to attack the enemy." Doles failed to mention that he displayed commendable initiative by attacking without waiting for orders.

Gordon's Georgians emerged from the willows lining Rock Creek to strike the defenders of Blocher's Knoll in the flank. On Gordon's orders, the troops marched slowly because they were much fatigued by the long march to the field. Gordon did not want them winded before they charged. The Brigade had to pass through some dangerous artillery fire. Then, when about 300 yards from the men of von Gilsa's Brigade, it charged.

Major-General Carl Schurz describes his plight.

0800 hrs	0900	1000	1100	1200	1300	1400	1500	1600	1700	1800
	pages 81-84						85-87	88-89		

51

"Suddenly the enemy opened upon the First Division from two batteries placed near the Harrisburg road, completely enfilading General Barlow's line...Soon afterward...the enemy appeared in our front with heavy masses of infantry, his line extending far beyond our right."

A close-range fire fight between Gordon's Brigade and von Gilsa's Brigade ensued. Gordon reported, "The enemy made a most obstinate resistance until the colors on portions of the two lines were separated by a space of less than 50 paces".

To meet the flank attack, the defenders futilely tried to change front. Meanwhile, Gordon rode just behind his lines to inspire his men. A rebel gunner saw Gordon "standing in his stirrups, bare-headed, hat in hand, arms extended...voice like a trumpet, exhorting his men." Sterling front-line leadership plus numbers and an advantageous tactical situation all favoured the Confederates. After a brief struggle, Gordon's charge drove von Gilsa's Brigade from the commanding knoll.

The defeated Union soldiers retired through the adjacent Union brigade commanded by Ames. Ames' Brigade was deployed at right angles to von Gilsa's Brigade and faced west. Gordon's Georgians pursued closely and struck Ames' flank before the yankees could prepare themselves. The Confederates delivered a terrible enfilade fire. Gordon relates Ames' response, "An effort was here made by the enemy to change his front and check our advance, but the effort failed, and this line, too, was driven back in the greatest confusion, and with immense loss in killed, wounded, and prisoners."

When Gordon's men struck Ames' right flank, Doles' Brigade crashed into Ames' left. The colonel of the 75th Ohio describes his men's plight: "Both flanks, being unsupported and exposed to an enfilading fire, were compelled to fall back with heavy loss in killed, wounded and missing."

After disposing of Ames' Brigade, Doles shifted his attention to Schimmelfennig's Division to the west. From Oak Hill, Carter's Artillery Battalion also targeted this Division. Doles managed to manoeuvre against the Union flank and send the yankees fleeing toward Gettysburg.

Meanwhile, the Federals retreating before Gordon tried to rally 500 yards to the rear by the Almshouse, on the northeast outskirts of Gettysburg. This was a superior position compared to the forward deployment at Blocher's Knoll. Here the Federals confronted continuing pressure from Gordon as well as the advance of Hays and Avery.

The peril of the Federal forward deployment lay in the ease with which their right flank could be turned. This is what Early set out to do with Hays' and Avery's Brigades. Initially, those two brigades had encountered resistance from Devin's Cavalry Brigade. They pushed aside these troopers and moved to assault Coster's Brigade at the Almshouse line. According to Early, they advanced "in fine style, encountering and driving (the enemy) back into the town in great confusion".

Indeed, Coster's men could not resist the combined weight of three Confederate brigades. After a brief combat, the rebels broke the Federal line. The Federals managed to discharge only six to nine volleys before retiring.

Once the surging Confederate line of infantry masked Jones' guns, the Confederate artillery displaced to the front. The Charlottesville Artillery moved across Rock Creek to protect the Division from any Federal attack directed against its left flank. The other three batteries advanced to positions from where they could fire against the yankees retreating into Gettysburg. But so quickly did the Union troops run that the guns never managed to fire before all targets were out of range.

Early's Division had performed superbly, inflicting three times as many losses as it suffered. The artillery had provided fine support with the Staunton Artillery firing 106 rounds, the Louisiana Guard Artillery 161, and the Courtney Artillery 595. The aggressive fire and mobile tactics displayed by these batteries and by Carter's Battalion had contributed to one of the finest days for Lee's 'Long Arm.'

The Division reported losses for July 1: Hays' Brigade lost 7 killed, 41 wounded, and 15 missing. Avery's Brigade lost 22 killed, 123 wounded, and no missing. Gordon's Brigade had carried the brunt of the fighting with 70 killed, 269 wounded, and 39 missing. Smith's Brigade remained unengaged. Doles' Brigade suffered most of its losses on July 1. For the entire battle it reported 24 killed, 124 wounded, and 31 missing.

In contrast to the earlier performances of several Confederate brigade commanders, the rebel leaders during this phase of the combat had shown well. Doles and Gordon were particularly notable. Rodes commended Doles' skilful leadership, reporting that he had handled his men with "marked coolness and courage." Gordon's conduct revealed him to be one of the army's rising stars.

0800 hrs	0900	1000	1100	1200	1300	1400	1500	1600	1700	1800
	pages 81-84						85-87	88-89		

II CORPS BATTLES
July 1 17.00 - 17.30 hrs

Pursuit

Early's appearance and Gordon's attack had acted as a signal for the entire Confederate line from the Hagerstown to the Heidlersburg road to advance. By 1630 hours, that advance had badly defeated both the Federal I and XI Corps. The success of the Confederate III Corps, coupled with the advance into Gettysburg from the north by II Corps, now provided the Confederate army with an opportunity and a decision. There was still ample daylight to achieve important results and fresh forces were soon to arrive. Everything hinged upon the judgment of the army's senior leaders.

Before these leaders could begin deliberations, their men performed an impetuous pursuit through the town of Gettysburg. From Seminary Ridge, Perrin's victorious soldiers pushed toward the town. Although

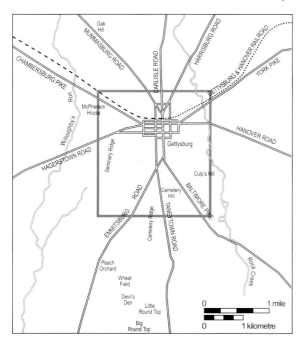

reduced by half, the 1st and 14th South Carolina chased the fleeing men of the Union I Corps. As they advanced they scooped up hundreds of prisoners, two field pieces, and a number of caissons. Just to their south, the 13th South Carolina easily drove down the slope of Seminary Ridge and across the open fields west of Gettysburg.

Once Perrin became convinced of the total defeat of the enemy, he regrouped his men. The brigades on either flank had not kept abreast of him. His Brigade alone lacked the strength to encircle the enemy from the south. He recalled the 1st and 14th, and sent a small provost party into town to collect prisoners. The Brigade's success had been great.

However, in his after-action report, Perrin dwelt on what had not been accomplished. As he was withdrawing his men toward Seminary Ridge the "first piece of artillery fired by the enemy from Cemetery Hill...was opened upon my command, and it was the same artillery which we had driven from our left near Gettysburg." Perrin believed that a better co-ordinated pursuit would have captured that artillery.

From north of Gettysburg, Doles' and Ramseur's Brigades also conducted a pursuit into the town. Doles reported, "We then moved rapidly by the left flank, to cut him off from the town. We did not succeed, as he retired faster than we advanced. We followed through the town as far as the outer edge of town, when I received an order to halt the column, and to form line of battle in the street running east and west through the town." Ramseur described much the same thing.

The troops in Pender's and Rodes' Divisions applied direct pressure against the fleeing Union troops. In contrast, by outflanking the far right of the Federal line, elements of Early's Division reached the town ahead of many of the retreating foe. Hays' Brigade was the principal pursuit force. Hays reported, "After reforming my

0800 hrs	0900	1000	1100	1200	1300	1400	1500	1600	1700	1800
	pages 81-84							85-87	88-89	

With the collapse of the Union resistance to the north of the town, the streets and narrow alleys of Gettysburg became a hunting ground as the Confederate troops pursued the fleeing Federals.

line of battle, I advanced through the city of Gettysburg, clearing it of the enemy and taking prisoners at every turn...unwilling to decrease my force by detailing a guard, I simply ordered them to the rear as they were taken. I am satisfied that the prisoners taken...exceeded in numbers the force under my command.

Trapped in Gettysburg's streets and alleys, thousands of Federal troops surrendered. A high proportion of the approximately 3,600 missing the Union army lost on July 1 occurred in the streets of Gettysburg. For perhaps 30 minutes, between 1615 and 1645 hours, Confederate soldiers gleefully hunted their enemy, chasing those who refused to surrender through yards, houses, and shops. One 16-year-old Georgia infantryman gathered up some 50 demoralised prisoners and presented them to his superiors.

At another point a Lieutenant Harvey of the 14th North Carolina captured the colours of the 150th Pennsylvania. Shortly thereafter, Harvey was mortally wounded. His last instructions were to hand over the flag, with his compliments, to Governor Zebulon Vance of North Carolina.

The joy of victory extended to General Gordon. While riding through Gettysburg's outskirts, an officer inquired, "General, where are your dead men?" Gordon replied, "I haven't any, Sir; the Almighty has covered my men with His shield and buckler!"

Despite the Confederate efforts to intercept the fleeing Union soldiers, the majority of the Federal I and XI Corps managed to pass through Gettysburg and reach Cemetery Hill. Here they encountered a reserve Brigade supported by artillery. If that dominating position was to be conquered, it would require one more assault.

From the perspective of corps commander Hill, the enemy had been entirely routed, but Heth and Pender were exhausted by hard fighting. He remarked to a British observer that the enemy had fought with unusual determination and inflicted severe losses. He later wrote, "Prudence led me to be content with what had been gained". This was far from the attitude that had brought Hill fame as commander of the Light Division.

Moreover, there were forces available to make another attack. Anderson's Division was rapidly approaching and two of Pender's brigades, Lane's and Thomas', had suffered light losses or not been engaged at all. There were also present numerous batteries that had yet to fire a shot. However, Hill was accompanied by General Lee and since Lee did not order him to prepare for another attack, Hill was satisfied to rest his men. If the high ground south of Gettysburg was to be attacked, it would be up to Ewell and his II Corps.

Some time after 1630 hours, Ewell rode through Gettysburg to examine Cemetery Hill. Early joined him here. Ewell had just about resolved to attack when Early received a message from Brigadier-General William Smith. Smith had remained in reserve back on the Harrisburg Pike. Here he believed he detected a large enemy force approaching from the east and reported this intelligence. Early told Ewell that he doubted it was true, but that it would be best to suspend any attack until he made certain the flank was secure.

Ewell concurred. In the meantime, he resolved to get Rodes into position and try to coordinate an attack with Hill. The courier sent to Hill returned to report that Hill would not advance, and that General Lee said he would leave it to Ewell's discretion whether to advance alone or not. If he discounted Smith's report of a threat to his rear, and that was by no means certain, Ewell could assemble three brigades belonging to Early and the three most intact brigades of Rodes for an evening assault.

These were men who had already marched a long distance earlier in the day. Half of them, the brigades

0800 hrs	0900	1000	1100	1200	1300	1400	1500	1600	1700	1800
	pages 81-84						85-87	88-89		

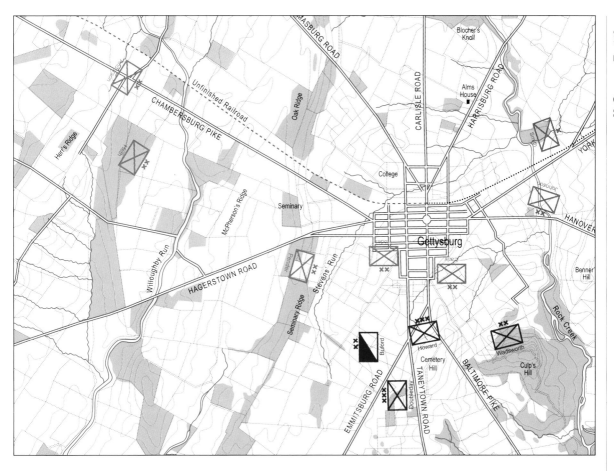

1630 hours - General Robert E. Lee's great dilemma; should he immediately attack Cemetery Hill or await the arrival of further components of his army. He chose the latter.

commanded by Daniel, Doles, and Gordon, had engaged in heavy combat. The assault troops would have to overcome significant obstacles. Units were intermingled in Gettysburg. The streets were clogged with both reforming Confederates and thousands of yankee prisoners.

The assault troops would have to move through Gettysburg and form at the base of Cemetery Hill. Here they would be vulnerable to the enemy artillery that was known to be on the heights. Lastly, and most important, no Confederate officer knew the strength of the Federal position on Cemetery Hill. Whatever its current strength, scouting officers could detect that it was increasing.

To General Lee's disappointment, Ewell decided not

to attack. Whether he could have done so would remain a hotly-debated topic, first among the veterans of the battle itself and later among students of Civil War history.

The Confederates had won a tactical victory on July 1, but it had been costly. In the attack against the Federal I Corps, Heth's, Pender's, and Rodes' Divisions had committed ten brigades. Seven of those brigades had suffered losses between 35% and 50%. Part of the explanation for this was that the attacks of both Heth and Pender had been piecemeal, while Rodes' initial effort had been horribly mismanaged by the brigade commanders. More importantly, the enemy had fought with skill and tenacity. By the time the fighting on July 1 ended, about 23,000 Confederate infantry had mastered the resistance of some 18,800 Union infantry and cavalry.

The striking power of three Confederate divisions was seriously reduced. In return, two Federal corps were shattered.

0800 hrs	0900	1000	1100	1200	1300	1400	1500	1600	1700	1800
	pages 81-84							85-87	88-89		

THE ARMY OF NORTHERN VIRGINIA

III CSA Army Corps

III Corps came into existence in the reorganisation following Jackson's death at Chancellorsville. Lee judged that its leader, A.P. Hill, had been his best divisional commander and encouraged his promotion to lieutenant-general. While the Corps was well pleased to have the magnetic, dashing Hill for its commander, the promotion of another Virginian annoyed other candidates who were not from Virginia.

Hill's old Light Division provided six of the Corps' thirteen brigades; two of them went to Heth's new Division and four to Pender's Division. To complete Heth's command, two brigades came from the Richmond defenses and the North Carolina littoral. The Corps' third division, commanded by Richard Anderson, had formerly served in Longstreet's I Corps. Consequently, III Corps had not yet forged team bonds and its commander and two of its divisional leaders were newly-promoted. Not only were its leaders unfamiliar with their subordinates, but Corps Commander Hill was enfeebled as he had begun to suffer from an unidentifiable illness.

On June 29 the Corps had received orders from Lee to move east of the mountains toward Cashtown in order to hold the enemy and prevent interruption of the army's lines of communication with Virginia.

June 30 found the Corps echeloned along the Chambersburg Pike from Cashtown, eight miles west of Gettysburg, toward Chambersburg. During the day, Brigadier-General Pettigrew took his command on a foraging expedition toward Gettysburg and encoun-

Lieutenant-General Ambrose Powell Hill, 37, graduated West Point and became a career soldier. During his Civil War service, he was popular with his men but plagued by ill health. His impetuosity served him well in only some of his battles.

tered opposition. He requested permission to return the following day. Heth, in turn, asked, "If there is no objection, I will take my Division tomorrow and go to Gettysburg." Hill replied, "None in the world." These casual words committed the Corps to a march that opened the Battle of Gettysburg.

---

15 Staff and Field Officers

III CORPS
Lieutenant-General Ambrose Powell Hill

Anderson's Division
Major-General Richard Heron Anderson
Heth's Division
Major-General Henry Heth/
Brigadier-General James Johnston Pettigrew
Pender's Division
Major-General William Dorsey Pender/
Brigadier-General James Henry Lane/
Major-General Isaac Ridgeway Trimble/
Brigadier-General James Henry Lane
III Corps Reserve Artillery
Colonel Reuben Lindsay Walker

III CSA Corps Casualties at Gettysburg 1st July 1863

Infantry killed or wounded	2,836
Infantry missing/captured	1,030
Artillery killed or wounded	34
Artillery missing/captured	10

III CSA ARMY CORPS - GETTYSBURG - July 1

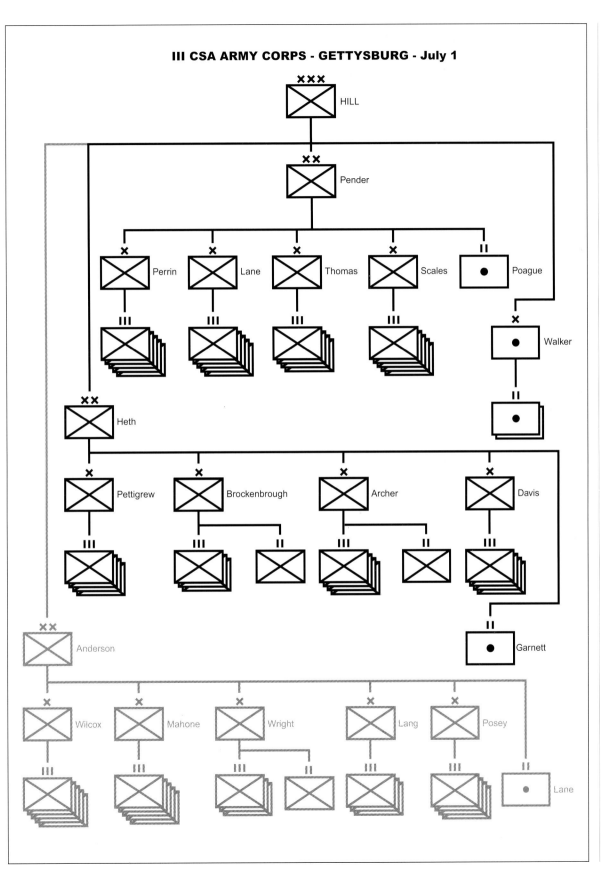

HILL

Pender

Perrin

Lane

Thomas

Scales

Poague

Walker

Heth

Pettigrew

Brockenbrough

Archer

Davis

Garnett

Anderson

Wilcox

Mahone

Wright

Lang

Posey

Lane

III CSA Army Corps - Anderson's Division

During Lee's reorganisation of the army after the Seven Days' Battles, the newly-promoted Major-General Richard Anderson assumed command of Major-General Benjamin Huger's former division. At that time the Division comprised three brigades, of which only Mahone's and Wright's were to be part of the organisation that Anderson commanded at Gettysburg.

Major-General Richard Heron Anderson, a 42-year old career soldier and West-Pointer, came from South Carolina. He was likeable and unassuming, but some said he lacked inner fire.

Assigned to Longstreet's Corps, Anderson's Division participated in the devastating assault that drove Pope's Federal army from the field. For the invasion of Maryland, three more brigades joined the Division.

> **ANDERSON'S DIVISION**
> *Major-General Richard Heron Anderson*
> **7 Staff and Field Officers**
>
> **Wilcox's Brigade 1,726**
> **Mahone's Brigade 1,542**
> **Wright's Brigade 1,413**
> **Perry's (Lang's) Brigade 742**
> **Posey's Brigade 1,322**
> **Lane's Artillery Battalion 384**

Those that would march to Gettysburg included: Wilcox's Brigade; three of the Mississippi regiments that would compose Posey's Brigade ; and two Florida and one Alabama regiment.

During the fighting at Sharpsburg, Anderson withdrew from the field with a painful wound. The Division, which until then had been fighting well, lost its drive, took heavy losses, and abandoned its position along Bloody Lane. Apparently Anderson's personal leadership had been instrumental in the Division's combat efficiency.

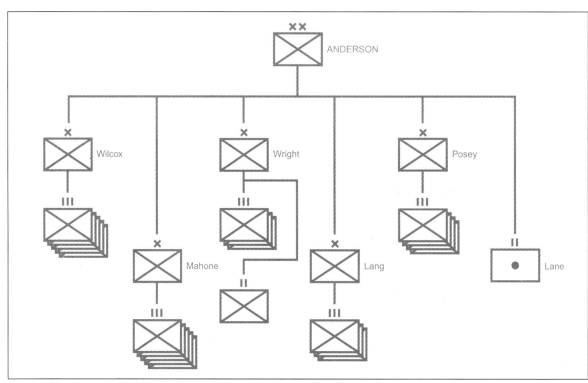

WILCOX'S BRIGADE
Brigadier-General Cadmus Marcellus Wilcox
5 Staff and Field Officers

8th Alabama Infantry Regiment
Lieutenant-Colonel Hilary Abner Herbert
477 troops present for duty equipped

11th Alabama Infantry Regiment
Colonel John Caldwell Calhoun Sanders
311 troops present for duty equipped

9th Alabama Infantry Regiment
Colonel Joseph Horace King
306 troops present for duty equipped

10th Alabama Infantry Regiment
Colonel William Henry Forney
311 troops present for duty equipped

14th Alabama Infantry Regiment
Colonel Lucius Pinckard
316 troops present for duty equipped

The State Flag of Alabama.

After Sharpsburg the entire army reorganised in order to have regiments of the same state grouped into brigades. At this time Anderson's Division assumed the structure with which it would march to Gettysburg. With soldiers representing five different states, it was one of the most diverse divisions in the army.

As one of the divisions Longstreet left behind with Lee while he embarked upon the Suffolk Campaign, Anderson's Division was active during the Chancellorsville Campaign. On May 1, 1863 the Division singlehandedly prevented the attempt by Hooker's Army of the Potomac to emerge from the Wilderness. The next day the Division maintained the Confederate right while Jackson manoeuvred around the Federal flank. On May 3, the Division made a heavy attack against the Fairview position. The following day it countermarched toward Fredericksburg to attack the Union's VI Corps. The Division lost 1,499 men killed, wounded, and missing during these engagements. The Division had fought well and its commander had demonstrated tactical competence. His performance caused Lee to call the 42-year-old general his "noble old general."

Officers and men liked "Dick" Anderson for his easy-going manners combined with military competence. When the army reorganised after Jackson's death, Anderson was a candidate for corps command. Instead he retained his division and saw it transferred

MAHONE'S BRIGADE
Brigadier-General William Mahone
4 Staff and Field Officers

6th Virginia Infantry Regiment
Colonel George Thomas Rogers
288 troops present for duty equipped

41st Virginia Infantry Regiment
Colonel William Allen Parham
276 troops present for duty equipped

12th Virginia Infantry Regiment
Colonel David Addison Weisiger
348 troops present for duty equipped

16th Virginia Infantry Regiment
Colonel Joseph Hutchinson Ham
270 troops present for duty equipped

61st Virginia Infantry Regiment
Colonel Virginius Despeaux Groner
356 troops present for duty equipped

WRIGHT'S BRIGADE
Brigadier-General Ambrose Ransom Wright
4 Staff and Field Officers

3rd Regiment Georgia Volunteer Infantry
Colonel Edward J. Walker
441 troops present for duty equipped

48th Regiment Georgia Volunteer Infantry
Colonel William Gibson
395 troops present for duty equipped

22nd Regiment Georgia Volunteer Infantry
Colonel Joseph Wasden
400 troops present for duty equipped

2nd Battalion Georgia Volunteer Infantry
Major George W. Ross
173 troops present for duty equipped

to A.P. Hill's newly-created III Corps. Anderson was accustomed to either Longstreet's firm control or Lee's close direction. However Hill commanded with a much looser rein and how the Division would perform under this novel situation was an open question.

Brigadier-General Cadmus Marcellus Wilcox, age 39, had been at the bottom of his class at West Point but returned to teach tactics. A dedicated career soldier, he was bitter about being passed over for promotion.

When the Gettysburg Campaign began, among Anderson's brigadiers, Cadmus Wilcox smouldered because he felt he had been passed over for promotion. Anderson judged William Mahone to be a "thorough disciplinarian and unites to military education great skill and untiring activity in the field." Ambrose Wright was solid but not particularly distinguished. He would not receive promotion until after departing the army in 1864. Carnot Posey first led his brigade at Chancellorsville where he particularly distinguished himself. Temporary brigade commander David Lang had been in three battles, two of which were as a captain.

The morning of July 1 found the Division at Fayetteville, 18 miles northwest of Gettysburg. Here it had enjoyed a three-day rest. However, its position at Fayetteville meant that it had the farthest distance to march of any of Hill's divisions. The Division formed road column by brigade with Wilcox's Brigade leading.

The Division's smallest brigade, led by Colonel David Lang, acting brigade commander in the absence of Brigadier-General Edward Perry who was ill with typhoid fever, served as rear guard.

The Division marched east over South Mountain to Cashtown, arriving between 1000 and 1100 hours. The men heard the sounds of combat but waited in Cashtown for some 90 minutes. Brigadier-General Ambrose Wright's Brigade had the luxury of bivouacking in a woodlot that shaded the soldiers from the hot July sun. Wright himself became indisposed and had to turn command over to his senior colonel, Gibson. Wright would return to duty at 0700 on July 2.

Meanwhile Anderson conferred with Lee. Ordered to march toward the sound of the guns, the Division found that congestion on the Chambersburg Pike made for slow progress. In order to have his available manpower concentrated, Anderson ordered Lang's Florida Brigade to cease rear guard duties, pass the Divisional trains, and close-up on the leading brigades.

Some time around 1700 the Division arrived on Herr

PERRY'S (LANG'S) BRIGADE
Colonel David Lang
3 Staff and Field Officers

2nd Florida Infantry Regiment
Major Walter Raleigh Moore
242 troops present for duty equipped

5th Florida Infantry Regiment
Captain Richmond N. Gardner
321 troops present for duty equipped

8th Florida Infantry Regiment
Lieutenant-Colonel William Baya
176 troops present for duty equipped

POSEY'S BRIGADE
Brigadier-General Carnot Posey
4 Staff and Field Officers

12th Mississippi Volunteer Infantry Regiment
Colonel William H. Taylor
305 troops present for duty equipped

19th Mississippi Volunteer Infantry Regiment
Colonel Nathaniel Harrison Harris
372 troops present for duty equipped

16th Mississippi Volunteer Infantry Regiment
Colonel Samuel E. Baker
385 troops present for duty equipped

48th Mississippi Volunteer Infantry Regiment
Colonel Joseph McAfee Jayne
256 troops present for duty equipped

Brigadier-General Carnot Posey, age 44, a gentleman planter and an honest lawyer in Mississippi, served in the Mexican War. His character and distinguished bearing impressed his superiors.

Ridge where it occupied the position formerly held by Pender's Division. Here it formed line of battle. The sounds of combat were clearly audible and some units caught glimpses of the fighting.

Obeying orders, Anderson sent Wilcox's Brigade and Ross' Company A Sumter Artillery a mile to the right where it took up a defensive position at a right angle to the Division's line near Black Horse Tavern. The order to halt surprised Anderson who rode ahead to confer again with Lee.

In a post-war conversation Anderson related that the "army was not all up, that he was in ignorance as to the force of the enemy in front" and that Anderson's Division, "alone of the troops present, had not been engaged, and that a reserve in case of disaster, was necessary."

With this statement, Lee overlooked the fast approach of Edward Johnson's Division. In any event, instead of assaulting Cemetery Hill, Anderson's Division, the largest in III Corps, remained positioned along Herr Ridge and did not see combat on July 1.

In his after-action report, Lee would write that he did not pursue the July 1 attacks because he worried about "exposing the four divisions present...to over-whelming numbers of fresh troops." Likewise, A.P. Hill wrote, "Under the impression that the enemy were entirely routed" and "my own two divisions exhausted by some six hours' hard fighting, prudence led me to be content with what had been gained, and not push forward." In fact as noted, Anderson's Division was available.

Divisional Artillery - Sumter (Georgia) Artillery (11th Georgia Battalion)
Major John Lane
9 Staff and Field Officers

Company A
Captain Hugh M. Ross
(130 troops present for duty equipped)
6 pieces

Company C
Captain John T. Wingfield
(121 troops present for duty equipped)
5 pieces

Company B
Captain George M. Patterson
(124 troops present for duty equipped)
6 pieces

III CSA Army Corps - Heth's Division

A triangular structure with three corps of three divisions each was devised by Lee when he reorganised the army after Chancellorsville. To accomplish this, the army needed a new division. Heth's Division became that unit.

It was formed from two brigades of A.P. Hill's old Light Division and two others that had been serving in the North Carolina littoral. The Light Division brigades, Archer's and Brockenbrough's, had the least distinguished reputations among Hill's original six brigades. Pettigrew's and Davis' Brigades included soldiers who had either never seen combat or had been but lightly

HETH'S DIVISION
Major-General Henry Heth/
Brigadier-General James Johnston Pettigrew
8 Staff and Field Officers

Pettigrew's Brigade 2,581
Brockenbrough's Brigade 971
Archer's Brigade 1,197
Davis' Brigade 2,305
Garnett's Artillery Battalion 396

Major-General Henry Heth, 37, graduated last in his class at West Point and became a career soldier. Ambrose Hill and he had been friends since their boyhood in Virginia. Heth owed his rapid advancement to his popularity among senior officers.

engaged. They were two of only four mixed-state brigades in the army. Their commander joined Lee's army early in 1863 to command Brockenbrough's Brigade. Because Heth was the senior brigadier, he briefly took command of Hill's Division at Chancellorsville when Hill was wounded. His seniority led to his promotion to major-general and divisional command. Gettysburg was Heth's first real battle experience as division commander.

Nightfall on June 30 found the Division at Cashtown. Although the least experienced division in the army, it would however open the battle because it was closest to the objective.

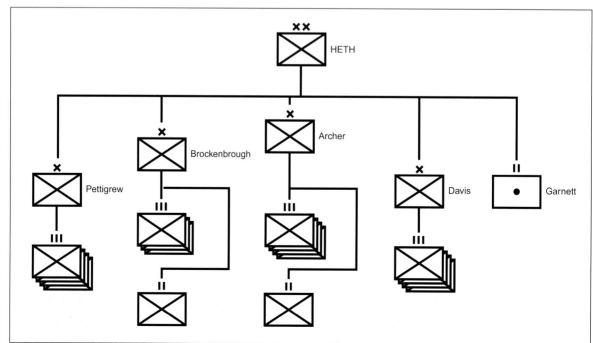

Heth's Division - Pettigrew's Brigade

After Chancellorsville, Lee's army sent two combat-depleted brigades to help defend North Carolina and received from that state two fresh

Brigadier-General James Johnston Pettigrew, 34, was an accomplished linguist, scholar, and lawyer from North Carolina who turned his intelligence to the pursuit of war. Gallant and self-effacing, he was revered by his men.

brigades. One of those was Pettigrew's North Carolina Brigade.

Previously the Brigade had seen little combat. Its commander was a brilliant scholar, a lawyer, and politician. Pettigrew had enlisted in Hampton's Legion as a private but had rapidly transferred to a North Carolina regiment that elected him Colonel. Since his near fatal wound at Seven Pines on May 31, 1862, Pettigrew had recovered and assumed brigade command.

Before being summoned to Virginia on May 30, 1863, the Brigade had operated in southern Virginia and North Carolina but had done little fighting. Pettigrew was popular among the Brigade because of his kind, and chivalrous nature. An officer said that he had "an

> ## PETTIGREW'S BRIGADE
> *Brigadier-General James Johnston Pettigrew/*
> *Colonel James Keith Marshall*

undoubted capacity to command" that obtained "instant obedience."

With more than 2,500 men, the Brigade was the largest in the army. It was logical to assign it to Heth's newly-formed Division. Because Pettigrew was the Division's senior brigadier, he would assume command if Heth fell, even though he was unfamiliar with both the Army of Northern Virginia and the other elements in the Division.

On June 30 the Brigade received orders "to march to Gettysburg, search the town for supplies (shoes especially) and return".

After marching the nine miles from Cashtown, the Brigade reached the outskirts of Gettysburg where it encountered Buford's cavalry. In addition, some officers believed that they had heard the sounds of drums

> ## 11th Regiment North Carolina Troops
> *Colonel Collett Leventhorpe*
> **Band**
> **617 troops present for duty equipped**
>
> **Cos. A thru K. *All Company names not available***

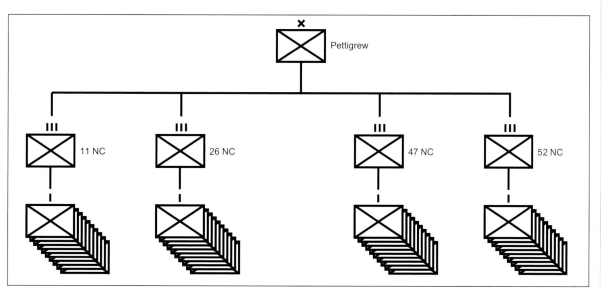

26th Regiment North Carolina Troops
Colonel Henry King Burgwyn, Jr./
Lieutenant-Colonel John Randolph Lane/
Major John Thomas Jones
Band
840 troops present for duty equipped

Co. A   Jeff Davis Mountaineers
Co. B   Waxhaw Jackson Guards
Co. C   Wilkes Volunteers
Co. D   Wake Guards
Co. E   Independent Guards
Co. F   Hibriten Guards
Co. G   Chatham Boys
Co. H   Moore Independents
Co. I   Caldwell Guards
Co. K   Pee Dee Wild Cats

The original battle flag of the 47th Regiment North Carolina Troops.

which suggested the presence of hostile infantry. Rather than bring on an engagement, Pettigrew ordered a withdrawal.

That evening, the Brigade maintained pickets about half way between Gettysburg and Cashtown on the Chambersburg Pike. When Heth's Division began its march the next day, July 1, Pettigrew's Brigade was third in the divisional column.

47th Regiment North Carolina Troops
Colonel George H. Faribault
567 troops present for duty equipped

Co. A   Chicora Guards
Co. B   *Name not available*
Co. C   *Name not available*
Co. D   Castalia Invincibles
Co. E   *Name not available*
Co. F   Sons of Liberty
Co. G   *Name not available*
Co. H   North Carolina Tigers
Co. I   *Name not available*
Co. K   Alamance Minute Men

52nd Regiment North Carolina Troops
Colonel James Keith Marshall/
Lieutenant-Colonel Marcus A. Parks
553 troops present for duty equipped

Co. A   Cabarrus Riflemen
Co. B   Randolph Guards
Co. C   Orapeake Guards
Co. D   McCulloch's Avengers
Co. E   Richmond Regulators
Co. F   Wilkes Grays
Co. G   Dry Pond Dixies
Co. H   Spring Hill Guards
Co. I   Stanly Rebels
Co. K   Fighting Boys

Heth's Division - Brockenbrough's Brigade

The four Virginia units serving in Brockenbrough's Brigade had had the misfortune of serving under a succession of temporary commanders for most of the year preceding the Gettysburg Campaign. The three regiments were veteran combat units. All had been raised in the summer of 1861. The three, but not the 22nd Battalion, served in the same brigade during the Seven Days' Battles. The Brigade suffered 580 casualties during this campaign.

In June of 1862, the 22nd Battalion, which had organised from the 2nd Artillery Regiment, joined the Brigade. It now had the composition with which it entered the Gettysburg Campaign. When its commander, Brigadier-General Charles Field, received a severe wound at the Battle of Second Manassas in

BROCKENBROUGH'S BRIGADE
Colonel John Mercer Brockenbrough
4 Staff and Field Officers

August 1862, Brockenbrough, by virtue of his seniority, assumed brigade command. The Brigade lost 95 men at Second Manassas.

Still referred to as "Field's Brigade," the Brigade continued under Brockenbrough's temporary leadership during the Invasion of Maryland where it saw only light combat. During the Fredericksburg Campaign in December 1862, the Brigade received a call to counter-attack to help seal a gap in the division's line.

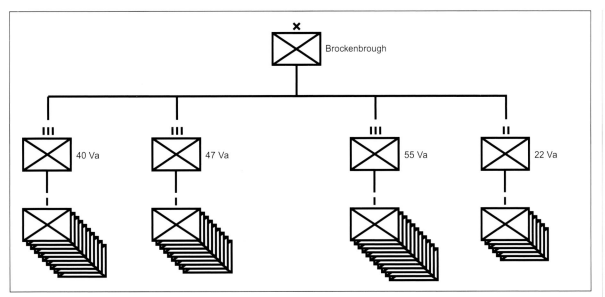

Brockenbrough lost control of his units. He led two regiments in the wrong direction and they never entered the fray. The brigade lost 83 men during this campaign.

Lee disliked having brigades led by temporary commanders and preferred promoting deserving colonels. Lee clearly judged Brockenbrough unworthy because in the spring of 1863, he imported Brigadier-General Henry Heth to command the brigade. During the Battle of Chancellorsville, Heth ascended to divisional command after A.P. Hill was wounded, and Brockenbrough returned to brigade command. For the first time under Brockenbrough's leadership, the Brigade performed respectably. On May 3 it stormed the Federal entrenchments defended by Sickle's III Corps and helped drive the Army of the Potomac into a defensive perimeter. Acting divisional commander Heth praised Brockenbrough's leadership during this battle.The entire campaign had been costly for the Brigade, losing 33 killed and 270 wounded though notably there were no men reported as missing. Among the killed

was the colonel of the 55th Virginia as well as the regiment's major while the lieutenant-colonel had been wounded.

Consequently, at the beginning of the Gettysburg Campaign the 55th was led by a new officer, Colonel William Christian. During the army's reorganisation in

47th Virginia Infantry Regiment
Colonel Robert Murphy Mayo
209 troops present for duty equipped

Co. A   Captain Charles J. Green's Co.
Co. B   CaptainEdward P. Tayloe's Co.
Co. C   Montross Guards
Co. D   Captain John W. Ltell's Co.
Co. E   Port Royal Guards
Co. F   Lacey Rifles
Co. H   Captain Thomas N. Welch's Co.
Co. I   Stafford Guards

40th Virginia Infantry Regiment
Captain Thomas Edwin Betts
253 troops present for duty equipped

Co. A   Wicomico Artillery
Co. B   Totuskey Grays
Co. C   Heathville Guards
Co. D   Farmer's Fork Grays
Co. E   Captain Thomas L. Pitt's Co.
Co. F   Captain Henry F. Cundiff's Co.
Co. G   Northumberland Rifles
Co. H   Lancaster Grays
Co. I   Robinson Guards
Co. K   Potomac Rifles

55th Virginia Infantry Regiment
Colonel William Steptoe Christian
268 troops present for duty equipped

Co. A   Essex Artillery
Co. C   Middlesex Southerners
Co. D   Essex Davis Rifles
Co. E   Westmoreland Grays
Co. F   Essex Sharpshooters
Co. G   Essex Greys
Co. H   Middlesex Rifles
Co. I   Captain Henry D. Barrick's Co.
Co. K   Captain William L. Broocke's Co.
Co. L   Captain Charles N. Lawson's Co.
Co. M   Captain John F. Alexander's Co.

the spring of 1863, the Brigade was removed from the Light Division and transferred, along with that division's other least distinguished brigade, to Heth's newly formed division. Again Lee declined to promote Brockenbrough. As the brigade marched north to Pennsylvania, it included veteran soldiers as good as any in the army. However, it had never regained the elan it had displayed when commanded by General Field. This can only be attributed to Brockenbrough's less than inspired leadership. Time would show that the colonel would never be promoted to general.

22nd Battalion Virginia Infantry
Major John Samuel` Bowles
237 troops present for duty equipped

Co. A Captain Thomas E. Burfoot's Co.
Co. B Charlotte and Luneburg Artillery
Co. D Captain Willian Green Jackson's Co.
Co. E Captain Robert Samuel Elam's Co.
Co. G Captain Kames C. Johnson's Co.
Co. H Captain John S. Bowles Co.

Heth's Division - Archer's Brigade

When a brigade composing three Tennessee, one Alabama, and one Georgia regiment lost its commander to a mortal wound at the Battle of Seven Pines on May 31, 1862, an obscure colonel named James Archer was promoted to brigadier-general and placed in command. Although

---

ARCHER'S BRIGADE
Brigadier-General James Jay Archer/
Colonel Birkett Davenport Fry/
Lieutenant-Colonel Samuel G. Shepard
4 Staff and Field Officers

Brigadier-General James Jay Archer was a 45-year-old Marylander who attended Princeton University. He served in the war in Mexico and rejoined the U.S. Army in 1855, serving until the outbreak of war.

Archer had served in the Mexican War and won a brevet for gallantry at the Battle of Chapultepec, he had little command experience. The Brigade, which at that time included four of the five units it would take to Gettysburg, did not like its new leader. They dubbed him "The Little Game Cock" for his irascible nature. The Brigade became the 5th Brigade in A.P. Hill's Light Division.

At the Battle of Mechanicsville the Brigade failed to penetrate a strong Union position. At Gaines' Mill it

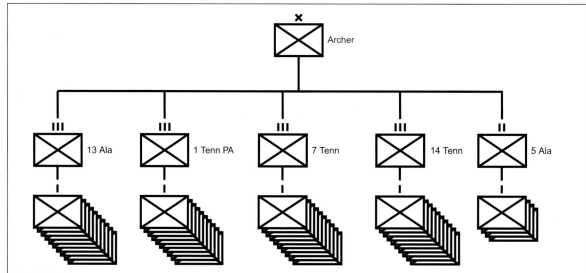

13th Alabama Infantry Regiment
Colonel Birkett Davenport Fry/
Lieutenent-Colonel James Aiken
308 troops present for duty equipped

Co. A Camden Rifles
Co. B Southern Stars
Co. C Alabama Borderers
Co. D Randolph Mountaineers
Co. E Randolph Rangers
Co. F Tallassee Guards
Co. G Yancey Guards
Co. H Coosa Mountaineers
Co. I Roanoke Mitchell Invincibles
Co. K Stephens Guards

7th Tennessee Infantry Regiment
Colonel John Amenas Fite
249 troops present for duty equipped

Co. A *Name not available*
Co. B *Name not available*
Co. C *Name not available*
Co. D Harris Rifles
Co. E *Name not available*
Co. F Statesville Tigers
Co. G Hurricane Rifles
Co. H The Grays
Co. I Silver Spring Guards
Co. K The Blues

charged to within 20 paces of the Federal line before being driven back with heavy losses. Because of Archer's conduct, the Brigade changed its view of him. He had "won the hearts of his men by his wonderful judgment and conduct on the field." He treated the

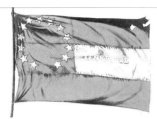

Battle flag of Colonel John Fite's 7th Tennessee Infantry Regiment.

5th Alabama Infantry Battalion
Major Albert Sebastian Van de Graaff
135 troops present for duty equipped

Co. A North Sumter Rifles
Co. B Calhoun Sharp Shooters
Co. C White Plains Rangers
Co. D Daniel Boone Rifles

humblest private with courtesy and henceforth the Brigade had "implicit confidence" in him.

The Brigade fought at Cedar Mountain and the Battle of Second Manassas where it saw heavy combat during the defence of the Railroad Cut. During the march to Sharpsburg, Archer had to turn command over to a

subordinate because of illness. He rallied, left his ambulance, and led the Brigade when it charged Burnside's penetration of Lee's right flank. After this performance, Archer had to relinquish command again the next day. At Chancellorsville, the Brigade reorganised into the same structure that it was to take to Gettysburg where it was one of only four mixed-states brigades. It became embroiled in the fighting around Catherine Furnace on May 2. The next day it captured the vital high ground at Hazel Grove.

Partially because Archer loathed Pender, the Brigade left the former Light Division and entered Heth's newly-formed division.

1st Tennessee Volunteer Infantry Regiment (Provisional Army)
Lieutenant-Colonel Newton J. George
281 troops present for duty equipped

Co. A Pelham Guards
Co. B Tullahoma Guards
Co. C Mountain Boys
Co. D Ridgedale Hornets
Co. E Lynchburg Rangers
Co. F Salem Invincibles
Co. G Fayetteville Guards
Co. H Shelton's Creek Volunteers
Co. I Tullahoma Guards
Co. K Boon's Creek Minutemen

14th Tennessee Infantry Regiment
Lieutenant-Colonel James William Lockert
220 troops present for duty equipped

Co. A *Name not available*
Co. B *Name not available*
Co. C Pepper Guards
Co. D *Name not available*
Co. E *Name not available*
Co. G *Name not available*
Co. H *Name not available*
Co. I *Name not available*
Co. K *Name not available*
Co. L *Name not available*

Heth's Division - Davis' Brigade

When Brigadier-General Joseph Davis' Brigade marched along the Chambersburg Pike toward Gettysburg on July 1, its 2,200 or so soldiers were being led into battle by an officer without combat experience. That inexperience was to have a devastating impact on the Brigade's fate.

The Brigade was one of four mixed-state units in the

Brigadier-General Joseph Robert Davis, 38, was Jefferson Davis' nephew and had neither military training nor combat experience when he approached Gettysburg.

Army of Northern Virginia during the Gettysburg Campaign. Half of the Brigade had an unsurpassed fighting record.

The 2nd and 11th Mississippi regiments formed in Corinth in April and May 1861, respectively. Both regiments rushed to Virginia to help defend that state from Federal invasion. The entire 2nd and two companies of the 11th fought in Brigadier-General Bee's Brigade at First Manassas.

Bee's Brigade was in the forefront of the fighting, losing a staggering 405 casualties, a total exceeded on

---

DAVIS' BRIGADE
Brigadier-General Joseph Robert Davis
6 Staff and Field Officers

---

that field only by the brigade commanded by Thomas Jackson.

With Bee's death at First Manassas, Brigadier-General William Whiting commanded the Brigade during the Peninsula Campaign. At the Battle of Seven Pines the Brigade was again in the heart of the fighting and suffered 346 casualties. During the ensuing Seven

---

2nd Mississippi Volunteer Infantry Regiment
Colonel John Marshall Stone/
Major John Alan Blair
492 troops present for duty equipped

Co. A   Tishomingo Riflemen
Co. B   O'Connor Rifles
Co. C   Town Creek Rifles
Co. D   Joe Matthews Rifles
Co. E   Calhoun Rifles
Co. F   Magnolia Rifles
Co. G   Pontotoc Minute Men
Co. H   Conewah Rifles
Co. I   Cherry Creek Rifles
Co. K   Iuka Rifles
Co. L   Liberty Guards

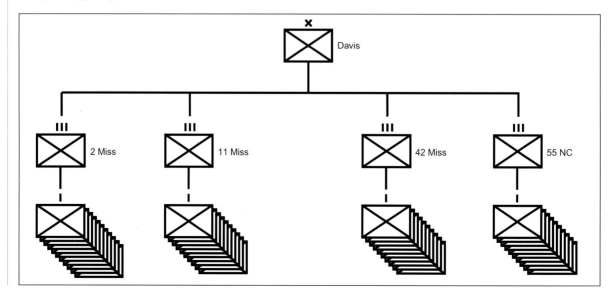

11th Mississippi Volunteer Infantry Regiment
Colonel Francis M. Green
592 troops present for duty equipped
(guarding divisional trains - not engaged)

Co. A   University Greys
Co. B   Coahoma Invincibles
Co. C   Prairie Rifles
Co. D   Neshoba Rifles
Co. E   Prairie Guards
Co. F   Van Dorn Reserves
Co. G   Noxubee Rifles
Co. H   Lamar Rifles
Co. I   Carroll Rifles
Co. K   Chickasaw Guards

42nd Mississippi Volunteer Infantry Regiment
Colonel Hugh Reid Miller
575 troops present for duty equipped

Co. A   Carroll Fencibles
Co. B   *Name not available*
Co. C   Nelson's Avengers
Co. D   *Name not available*
Co. E   Davenport Rifles
Co. F   *Name not available*
Co. G   Gaston Rifles
Co. H   *Name not available*
Co. I   Mississippi Reds
Co. K   *Name not available*

The original battle flag of the 11th Mississippi Volunteer Infantry Regiment.

Days' Battles, the Brigade endured more heavy losses, losing 553 men. At these battles, Colonel John Stone commanded the 2nd Mississippi. He was also to lead the regiment at Gettysburg.

After the reorganisation before the Second Manassas Campaign, the Brigade found itself in Brigadier-General John Hood's Division. Hood was never one to shirk combat. Consequently, the Brigade engaged heavily at the Battle of Second Manassas where it lost 324 men.

Sharpsburg was worse. The combat around the Corn Field cost the Brigade severely. During the Invasion of Maryland it lost 468 casualties including a wound to Colonel Stone. The lieutenant-colonel of the 11th Mississippi also was wounded while that unit's colonel received a mortal wound. These two battered regiments temporarily departed the army after Sharpsburg.

In contrast to the 2nd and 11th Mississippi regiments, both the 42nd Mississippi and the 55th North Carolina were green regiments, formed in summer of 1862. Unlike the more highly motivated early war volunteers, their ranks included many conscripted soldiers or men who had joined under the threat of conscription.

The three Mississippi regiments merged into a brigade that first saw joint service in North Carolina. Here, in January 1863, Mississippi native Joseph Davis, the Confederate President's nephew, assumed command. His position was due to pure nepotism. Having never directed troops in battle, Davis received a promotion to brigadier-general in September 1862.

While in North Carolina, the 55th North Carolina joined the brigade. By Confederate standards of 1863, all four regiments were numerically strong with the 55th contributing the most men to the Brigade's strength. The Brigade participated in Longstreet's Suffolk Campaign and then moved north to join the main army after the Chancellorsville Campaign. Here, this unique brigade joined Major-General Henry Heth's newly formed division.

The Brigade marched second in Heth's column on the road to Gettysburg. The veteran 11th Mississippi was detached and left behind to guard the divisional trains. An observer had described the Brigade's leader as "a very pleasant and unpretending gentleman." Whether he had the stuff to lead his brigade effectively in battle was about to be tested.

55th Regiment North Carolina Troops
Colonel John Kerr Connally/
Lieutenant-Colonel Maurice T. Smith/
Major Alfred H. Belo/
Captain George Gilreath
640 troops present for duty equipped

Co. A   *Name not available*
Co. B   *Name not available*
Co. C   Cleveland Grays
Co. D   Cleveland Farmers
Co. E   *Name not available*
Co. F   South Mountain Rangers
Co. G   North Carolina Rebels
Co. H   Alexander Boys
Co. I   Franklin Farmers
Co. K   *Name not available*

Heth's Division - Garnett's Artillery Battalion

After Chancellorsville, Garnett's Artillery Battalion was assigned to provide fire-support for Heth's newly-formed division. The Battalion was led by a West Point trained officer whose war-time career to date had included service with the Washington Artillery Battalion, Divisional Chief of Artillery, and Inspector of Ordnance and Artillery in Longstreet's Corps. Garnett was recognised as an efficient artillery officer.

The Battalion's four batteries were veteran outfits. The Norfolk Light Artillery Blues originated in 1829. It consistently attracted that city's "young Gentlemen" up to its entrance into the Confederate army in 1861. The

The 12-pounder howitzer fired a shell to a range of between 195 and 1,072 yards. It fired canister for close-range, anti-personnel work. By November 1862, no more of these howitzers were manufactured in the South with many existing models being melted to recast 12-pounder Napoleons.

Divisional Artillery
Lieutenant-Colonel John Jameson Garnett
9 Staff and Field Officers

Huger Battery formed on June 8, 1861 from extra men belonging to Grandy's Norfolk Battery. It derived its name from its first captain, Frank Huger, the son of departmental commander General Benjamin Huger. On March 2, 1863, Huger received a promotion and Lieutenant Joseph Moore ascended to battery command.

The Louisiana Battery, the Donaldsonville Artillery, also had a long history dating back to its formation in 1837. It had served in Virginia since 1861.

The Battalion was actively engaged during the Chancellorsville Campaign where it served with Anderson's Division. It lost about 25 casualties. After the battle the Battalion received 26 horses to replace partially those that had been lost.

The Battalion began its march north on June 15, 1863. It passed through Chester Gap to enter the Shenandoah Valley and crossed the Potomac River On June 25. Arriving at Cashtown on June 29 after a tiring march, the Battalion enjoyed a day of rest on June 30. Observing the growing concentration of man-

power from Chambersburg to Cashtown, a battery gunner remarked that "everything last night wore the appearance of battle."

Garnett's Battalion of Artillery

Donaldsonville Artillery (Louisiana)
Captain Victor Maurin
(114 troops present for duty equipped)
2 3-inch rifled guns
1 10-pounder Parrott rifled gun

Huger Battery (Virginia)
Captain Joseph D. Moore
(77 troops present for duty equipped)
1 3-inch rifled guns
1 10-pounder Parrott rifled gun

Lewis Artillery (Virginia)
Captain John W. Lewis
(90 troops present for duty equipped)
2 3-inch rifled guns
2 12-pounder Napoleon guns

Norfolk Light Artillery Blues (Virginia)
Captain Charles R. Grandy
(106 troops present for duty equipped)
2 3-inch rifled gun
2 12-pounder howitzers

BATTALION EQUIPMENT

17 Caissons
159 Horses
4 Forges
1 Battery Wagon

III CSA Army Corps - Pender's Division

In the army-wide reorganisation after Chancellorsville, the obvious candidate for restructuring was A.P. Hill's six-brigade Light Division. Upon his promotion to corps command, Hill pondered who should be promoted to command his former division. Hill recommended General William Pender, who previously had led a brigade within the division. Pender's Brigade had been the most efficient unit in the excellent division. Hill wanted to preserve its "pride in its name...its

> **PENDER'S DIVISION**
> *Major-General William Dorsey Pender*
> **11 Staff and Field Officers**
>
> **Perrin's Brigade 1,882**
> **Lane's Brigade 1,734**
> **Thomas' Brigade 1,326**
> **Scales' Brigade 1,351**
> **Poague's Artillery Battalion 377**

Major-General William Dorsey Pender, a 29-year-old from North Carolina, was a West Point graduate and career soldier. The former dragoon and artilleryman displayed great battlefield courage which won him rapid promotion in the Confederate army.

26, 1862. It pressed the attack the next day at Gaines' Mill and again three days later at Frayser's Farm. At Cedar Mountain on August 9, its fast march and rapid deployment on the field saved Stonewall Jackson from defeat. The Division defended Jackson's left at Second Manassas and fought at Chantilly on September 1. After participating in the capture of Harper's Ferry, it performed an epic route march to Sharpsburg where it arrived in late afternoon in time to drive back the Federal left flank and save Lee's army. At Chancellorsville it participated in Jackson's tremendous flank assault and the next day assaulted the Union perimeter at Fairview.

During the invasion of Pennsylvania, Pender's Division proudly wore the mantle of Hill's old Light Division and rightfully considered itself as the Corps' shock troops. At age 29, their commander was the youngest major-general in the army and a rising star.

The Division camped at Cashtown on the night of June 30.

'shoulder to shoulder feeling' and good feelings between brigades." Lee concurred.

Pender's Division composed the four best brigades from A.P. Hill's old Light Division. They had been united as a team through a spectacularly successful year of victory. The Division opened Lee's Seven Days' offensive when it attacked at Mechanicsville on June

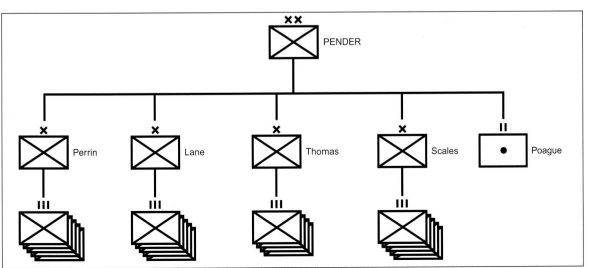

Pender's Division - Perrin's Brigade

As one of only two South Carolina brigades in the Army of Northern Virginia, Colonel Abner Perrin's Brigade carried a proud reputation. It had earned renown under the command of Brigadier-General Maxey Gregg during the Seven Days' Battles.

Composed of some of the finest soldiers South Carolina had to contribute to the cause, its regiments included men from the 1st Volunteers who formed the 1st Regiment, Provisional Army, as well as the 1st

casualties was Lieutenant-Colonel Perrin, who received a wound.

At Fredericksburg the brigade lost its fearless leader Gregg among its 363 casualties. The Brigade's senior

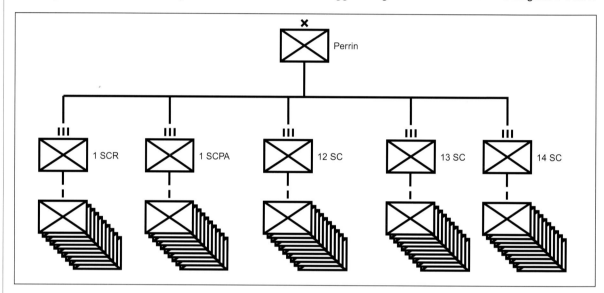

Rifles, the so called "Orr's Rifles." From Seven Days' on, the Brigade had the same organisation it was to have at Gettysburg. As part of A.P. Hill's Light Division, it suffered dearly at Gaines' Mill and Glendale, losing 929 men.

It took part in all of the Light Division's exploits during the remainder of 1862. In furious fighting, the Brigade suffered another 722 casualties at Second Manassas. After participating in the capture of Harper's Ferry, it conducted the speed march to Sharpsburg where it pitched in against the Federal left flank. Among its 165

colonel, Samuel McGowan, took over leadership while Perrin became commander of the 14th South Carolina.

Promoted to full colonel in January 1863, Perrin led his regiment during the Chancellorsville Campaign. Fighting with its customary elan, the Brigade partici-

1st South Carolina Regiment (Provisional Army)
Major Comillus Wycliffe McCreary
328 troops present for duty equipped

Co. A Gregg Guard
Co. B Rhett Guard
Co. C Richland Rifles
Co. E *Name not available*
Co. F Horry Rebels
Co. G Butler Sentinels
Co. H *Name not available*
Co. I *Name not available*
Co. K *Name not available*
Co. L Carolina Light Infantry

1st South Carolina Rifles (Orr's Regiment of Rifles)
Captain William M. Hadden
366 troops present for duty equipped

Cos. A thru H and K and L.
All Company names unavailable

12th South Carolina Volunteer Regiment
Colonel John Lucas Miller
366 troops present for duty equipped

Co. A *Name not available*
Co. B *Name not available*
Co. C *Name not available*
Co. D *Name not available*
Co. E *Name not available*
Co. F *Name not available*
Co. G Bonham Rifles Volunteers
Co. H *Name not available*
Co. I *Name not available*
Co. K *Name not available*

Light Division to be assigned to Pender's Division in the army's reorganisation after Chancellorsville. It was one of the army's premier brigades. However, so severe had been its cumulative losses that it was led north to Gettysburg by an officer who had yet to be mentioned in dispatches or to receive any particular commendation.

Its regiments were commanded by men who had risen through attrition. Only one of its five units was commanded by a full colonel. Given its inexperienced leadership, how it would uphold its tradition was yet another of the army's open questions.

On July 1, Perrin's Brigade was the vanguard of Pender's Division as it marched through Cashtown Gap toward the sounds of battle.

pated in Jackson's flank attack against Howard's XI Corps at Chancellorsville. The Brigade suffered 455 casualties, one of which was McGowan who was severely wounded. Perrin therefore ascended to brigade command.

The brigade was one of the chosen four from the old

14th South Carolina Volunteer Regiment
Lieutenant-Colonel Joseph Newton Brown
428 troops present for duty equipped

Co. A Lynch Creek Guards
Co. B Dearing Guards
Co. C Raiborn Co.
Co. D Edgefield Rifles
Co. E Enoree Mosquitos
Co. F Carolina Bees
Co. G *Name not available*
Co. H Ryan's Guards
Co. I McCalla Rifles
Co. K Meeting Street Saludas

13th South Carolina Volunteer Regiment
Lieutenant-Colonel Benjamin Thomas Brockman
390 troops present for duty equipped

Cos. A thru K. *All Company names not available*

Pender's Division - Lane's Brigade

Brigadier-General James Henry Lane graduated from both the Virginia Military Institute and the University of Virginia before returning to teach at VMI, and then the North Carolina Military Institute. He was 31 in 1863.

After the Battle of Sharpsburg, when the soldiers in Branch's Brigade petitioned to select a new commander to replace the fallen Brigadier-

LANE'S BRIGADE
Brigadier-General James Henry Lane
4 Staff and Field Officers

General Lawrence Branch, they nominated James Henry Lane. Known as "Little Jim", Lane was one of the army's intellectual soldiers having attended and then instructed at the Virginia Military Institute. He went on to teach military tactics at the North Carolina Military Institute. Although a native Virginian, Lane had served with his cadets at the outbreak of war where they fought and won the first battle in the East on June 10, 1861 at Big Bethel. Lane ascended to Colonel of the 28th North Carolina and served in this capacity during the Seven Days' Battles. Brigade commander Branch cited Lane first when he commended deserving offi-

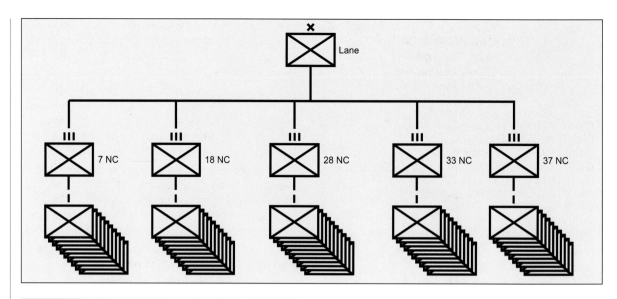

7th North Carolina State Troops
Captain J. McLeod Turner
291 troops present for duty equipped

Co. A *Name not available*
Co. B *Name not available*
Co. C *Name not available*
Co. D *Name not available*
Co. E *Name not available*
Co. F *Name not available*
Co. G **Wake Rangers**
Co. H *Name not available*
Co. I *Name not available*
Co. K *Name not available*

cers after that campaign.

As part of A.P. Hill's Light Division, the Brigade fought along the Railroad Cut at Second Manassas. It participated in the capture of Harper's Ferry and then rapidly marched to Sharpsburg on September 17, 1862. It pitched in, along with the Light Division's

other brigades, to savage Burnside's Corps and help save Lee's army in the late hours of the Battle of Sharpsburg.

Here Branch fell while leading a charge and Lane took temporary command. Lee accepted the soldiers' petition and promoted Lane to brigadier-general on November 1, 1862.

The five regiments composing the Brigade were experienced soldiers. The 7th North Carolina State Troops had formed in August 1861. The 18th formed in June 1861. The 28th, Lane's old regiment, formed in

The original battle flag of Colonel Samuel Lowe's 28th Regiment North Carolina Troops.

18th Regiment North Carolina Troops
Colonel John Decatur Barry
346 troops present for duty equipped

Co. A **German Volunteers**
Co. B **Bladen Light Infantry**
Co. C **Columbus Guards**
Co. D **Robeson Light Infantry**
Co. E **Moore's Creek Riflemen**
Co. F **Scotch Boys**
Co. G **Wilmington Light Infantry**
Co. H **Columbus Vigilants**
Co. I **Wilmington Rifle Guards**
Co. K **Bladen Guards**

28th Regiment North Carolina Troops
Colonel Samuel D. Lowe
346 troops present for duty equipped

Co. A **Surry Regulators**
Co. B **Gaston Invincibles**
Co. C **South Fork Farmers**
Co. D **Stanly Yankee Hunters**
Co. E **Montgomery Grays**
Co. F **Yadkin Boys**
Co. G **Guards of Independence**
Co. H **Cleveland Regulators**
Co. I **Yadkin Stars**
Co. K **Stanly Guards**

33rd Regiment North Carolina State Troops
Colonel Clark Moulton Avery
368 troops present for duty equipped

Co. A *Name not available*
Co. B Clark's Guards
Co. C Cabarrus Hornets
Co. D Wilkes Regulators
Co. E *Name not available*
Co. F Dixie Invincibles
Co. G Cumberland Rangers
Co. H *Name not available*
Co. I Confederate Stars
Co. K *Name not available*

37th Regiment North Carolina Troops
Colonel William M. Barbour
379 troops present for duty equipped

Co. A Ashe Beauregard Riflemen
Co. B Watauga Marksmen
Co. C Mecklenburg's Wide Awakes
Co. D North Carolina Defenders
Co. E Watauga Minute Men
Co. F Western Carolina Stars
Co. G Alexander Soldiers
Co. H Gaston Blues
Co. I Mecklenburg Rifles
Co. K Alleghany Tigers

September 1861. The 33rd formed in September 1861 while the 37th formed in November of that year. The Brigade was one of the charter members of A.P. Hill's Light Division.

During the Seven Days' Battles it had suffered the staggering total of 105 killed, 706 wounded, and only 28 missing. Exhibiting front-line leadership, the colonel of the 7th had been killed and the colonel of the 37th wounded.

At the Battle of Fredericksburg, Lane's first as brigade commander, the Brigade had the misfortune to leave its right flank unprotected. When Meade's Federal troops drove past this flank, Lane maintained his composure and handled the Brigade with skill until reinforcements sealed the breach. At Fredericksburg, the Brigade suffered 535 casualties, the highest total among Hill's six brigades.

During the Chancellorsville Campaign, the Brigade was in the forefront of Stonewall Jackson's flank attack. Here it lost 909 men, a total higher than that suffered by any other brigade in either army. The 33rd alone lost 41 percent of its strength. To its eternal chagrin, it then tarnished its glory when nervous soldiers of the 18th North Carolina fired a volley that gave Jackson his mortal wound on May 2, 1863.

The Brigade camped on the north side of South Mountain on June 30. It began its march to Gettysburg the next day at 0800. Lane was the Division's senior brigadier.

Pender's Division - Thomas' Brigade

While serving in A.P. Hill's Light Division, Edward Thomas' leadership had attracted favourable attention when his 35th Georgia had been the only unit to fight its way across Beaver Dam Creek. At the end of the Seven Day's Battles, when General Joseph Anderson retired to manage

Brigadier-General Edward Lloyd Thomas, 38, from Georgia, spent much of his life as a gentleman planter, interrupted by military service in the Mexican War. By Gettysburg, he had performed solidly as a brigadier.

THOMAS' BRIGADE
Brigadier-General Edward Lloyd Thomas
4 Staff and Field Officers

Richmond's Tredegar Iron Works, Thomas replaced him. It began an association between this Georgia brigade and Thomas that lasted for the remainder of the war.

The Second Manassas Campaign marked the Brigade's debut under Thomas. At Cedar Mountain it fought well and at Second Manassas it tenaciously defended its position along the Railroad Cut. The Brigade missed Sharpsburg since it was left behind at Harper's Ferry to parole Federal prisoners. At Fredericksburg it counter-attacked Meade's penetration of Hill's line. During the Chancellorsville Campaign

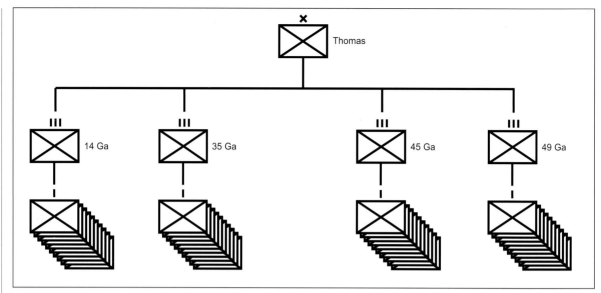

it trailed Jackson's column during his famous flank march and became delayed by the fight around Catherine Furnace. Consequently, it suffered the least of any of the Light Division units during the battle.

As the Brigade marched into Pennsylvania, it carried

14th Regiment Georgia Volunteer Infantry
Colonel Robert Warren Folsom
331 troops present for duty equipped

Co. A Confederate Volunteers
Co. B Ramah Guards
Co. C Jasper Light Infantry
Co. D Cherokee Brown Rangers
Co. E Lester Volunteers
Co. F Johnson Greys
Co. G Yancey Independents
Co. H Blackshear Guards
Co. I   Jeff Davis Riflemen
Co. K Etowah Guards

35th Regiment Georgia Volunteer Infantry
Lieutenant-Colonel William Henry McCullohs
331 troops present for duty equipped

Co. A Brown Guards
Co. B Bartow Avengers
Co. C Campbell Rangers
Co. D *Name not available*
Co. E Campbell Volunteers
Co. F *Name not available*
Co. G Walton Sharpshooters
Co. H County Line Invincibles
Co. I   Chattooga Mountaineers
Co. K Harris Guards

45th Regiment Georgia Volunteer Infantry
Lieutenent-Colonel Washington Leonidas Grice
331 troops present for duty equipped

Co. A Gresham Rifles
Co. B Rutland Volunteers
Co. C Dooly Volunteers
Co. D McCowan Guard
Co. E Taylor Volunteers
Co. F Gray Volunteers
Co. G Myrick Volunteers
Co. H Henderson Rangers
Co. I   Byars Volunteers
Co. K Ray Guards

a solid, if not flashy, reputation and could accurately boast that it had never been driven from any position. It accompanied Pender's Division to Gettysburg and arrived on Herr Ridge shortly before 1200 hours.

49th Regiment Georgia Volunteer Infantry
Colonel Samuel Thomas Player
329 troops present for duty equipped

Co. A Wilkinson Invincibles
Co. B Telfair Volunteers
Co. C Washington Guards
Co. D Taliaferro Volunteers
Co. E States Rights Guards
Co. F Irwin Volunteers
Co. G Laurens Volunteers
Co. H Cold Steel Guards
Co. I   Pierce Guards
Co. K Pulaski Greys

Pender's Division - Scales' Brigade

The five North Carolina regiments composing Scales' Brigade were as fine troops as any in the Army of Northern Virginia. Division leader Major-General Dorsey Pender took particular interest in the Brigade since it had been his old command. During the time the brigade had been associated with A.P. Hill's Light Division, Hill had called the unit "the best drilled and disciplined Brigade in the Division."

The 13th, 16th, and 22nd regiments formed in the summer of 1861 as part of the first wave of volunteer units to enter North Carolina service. The 34th also benefited from the first flush of patriotic enthusiasm and formed in the field in October 1861. Pender was the first colonel of the 13th Regiment. One of that

regiment's captains was Alfred Scales, a prominent state politician who unlike many of his ilk had not lobbied for an officer's commission but rather had enlisted as a private. When Pender transferred to the 6th North Carolina , Scales succeeded him as colonel.

The 13th first saw combat at the Battle of

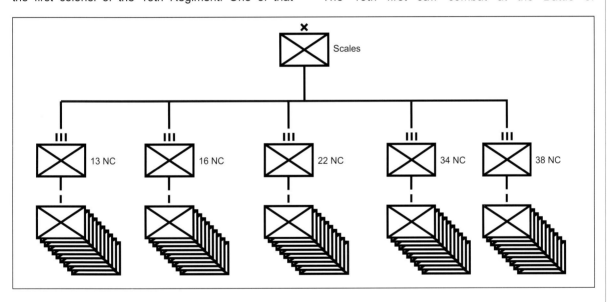

13th Regiment North Carolina Troops
Colonel Joseph Henry Hyman/
Lieutenant-Colonel Henry A. Rogers/
Lieutenent Robert L. Moir
232 troops present for duty equipped

Co. A   Yanceyville Grays
Co. B   Ranaleburg Riflemen
Co. C   Milton Blues
Co. D   Leasburg Grays
Co. E   Alamance Regulators
Co. F   Davie Grays
Co. G   Edgecombe Rifles
Co. H   Rockingham Guards
Co. I   Rockingham Rangers
Co. K   Dixie Boys

Williamsburg in early May 1862. The regiment also fought at Mechanicsville, Gaines' Mill, and Malvern Hill. During these actions, Scales provided conspicuous, front-line leadership. With Scales absent because of illness, the regiment participated in the Maryland Campaign.

The other regiments belonged to Pender's Brigade, one of the original elements of the Light Division. During the Seven Days' Battles, Pender's Brigade included the 16th, 22nd, and 34th North Carolina along with an Arkansas and a Virginia unit. The Brigade fought ferociously and lost more than 800 men.

Reorganised into an all-North Carolina brigade with the addition of the recently mustered 38th, the unit was lightly engaged at the Battle of Cedar Mountain and

16th Regiment North Carolina Troops
Captain Leroy W. Stowe
321 troops present for duty equipped

Co. B *Name not available*
Co. C *Name not available*
Co. D *Name not available*
Co. E **Burke Tigers**
Co. F *Name not available*
Co. G *Name not available*
Co. H *Name not available*
Co. I *Name not available*
Co. K *Name not available*
Co. M *Name not available*

34th Regiment North Carolina Troops
Colonel William Lee Joshua Lowrance/
Lieutenant-Colonel George T. Gordon
311 troops present for duty equipped

Co. A **Laurel Spring Guard**
Co. B **Sandy Run Yellow Jackets**
Co. C **Rutherford Rebels**
Co. D **Oakland Guards**
Co. E **Shady Grove Rangers**
Co. F **Floyd Rifles**
Co. G **Mecklenburg Boys**
Co. H **Rough and Readys**
Co. I **Rutherford Band**
Co. K **Montgomery Boys**

Brigadier-General Alfred Moore Scales, 45, had been a lawyer and U.S. legislator before enlisting as a private in the Confederate army. Gallant in battle, he rose rapidly through the ranks.

a commendation.

Pender recovered to lead the brigade in the Chancellorsville Campaign during which it suffered 116 killed, 567 wounded, and 68 missing. These heavy losses included wounds to Scales, who remained on the field until forced to leave from blood loss, the colonel and lieutenant-colonel of the 16th, and the death of the 22nd's lieutenant-colonel. These casualties degraded regimental command.

In the reorganisation after Chancellorsville, the four select brigades from the old Light Division became Pender's Division. With Pender promoted to Major-General, Scales received promotion to Brigadier-General on June 13. In turn, the 13th's former Lieutenant-Colonel, Joseph Hyman, was promoted to full Colonel. For the march north to Gettysburg the Brigade was consequently led by a newly appointed Brigadier; the 13th by a recently promoted Colonel, and the 16th by that regiment's senior Captain. Consistancy of command therefore suffered.

fought at Second Manassas where it lost 223 men. Pender's Brigade was not as heavily engaged as other Light Division brigades at Sharpsburg, where it suffered only 30 casualties.

With the transfer of the 13th, the Brigade fought at Fredericksburg with the same organisation it was to have at Gettysburg. Among its 169 casualties was Pender, who was wounded.

Although a newcomer to the brigade, Scales was the senior colonel. Accordingly, he commanded the Brigade for the later portions of this battle and received

22nd Regiment North Carolina Troops
Colonel James Conner
267 troops present for duty equipped

Co. A **Caldwell Rough and Ready Boys**
Co. B **McDowell Rifles**
Co. E **Guilford Men**
Co. F **Alleghany True Blues**
Co. G **Caswell Rifles**
Co. H **Stokes Boys**
Co. I **Davis Guards**
Co. K **McDowell Boys**
Co. L **Uwharrie Rifles**
Co. M **Randolph Hornets**

38th Regiment North Carolina Troops
Colonel William J. Hoke/
Lieutenant-Colonel John Ashford/
Captain William L. Thornburg/
Lieutenant John M. Robinson
216 troops present for duty equipped

Co. A **Spartan Band**
Co. B **Men of Yadkin**
Co. C **Sampson Farmers**
Co. D **Sampson Plowboys**
Co. E **Richmond Boys**
Co. F **Catawba Wildcats**
Co. G **Rocky Face Rangers**
Co. H **Uwharrie Boys**
Co. I **Cleveland Marksmen**
Co. K **Carolina Boys**

Pender's Division - Poague's Artillery Battalion

In the army-wide reorganization after Chancellorsville, Poague's Battalion was newly formed to provide fire support for Pender's Division. The four batteries had never worked together before. Captain Graham's North Carolina battery had served with the army during the Seven Days' Battles in 1862 but thereafter had been on detached duty. The Madison Light Artillery was an inexperienced battery, having been formed in Mississippi in the spring of 1863. The Battalion's two Virginia batteries were more experienced. Captain Brooke's battery had formed in March 1862 and seen continual service with the Army of Northern Virginia beginning with the Fredericksburg Campaign. Captain Wyatt's battery had formed in June 1861 and served with the army until July 1862 before rejoining the army in June 1863.

The battalion commander, Major William T. Poague, was a veteran artilleryman. He began his war service when elected lieutenant of the 1st Rockbridge Artillery in the spring of 1861. He was elected battery captain in April 1862 and remained in that position until promoted to major the following year. In February 1863, General Pendleton described Poague as "a superior officer, whose services have been scarcely surpassed." The Gettysburg Campaign would be Poague's first as a battalion commander.

Because most battery commanders preferred to retain the types of artillery pieces with which they were most familiar, Pendleton's efforts to standardize tube types had not been pressed. Consequently, Poague's Battalion had a mixture of pieces which increased the problems of ammunition supply and impaired the Battalion's general efficiency.

The Battalion, with three batteries, departed Fredericksburg on June 15, 1863. Reaching Culpeper Court House two days later, it was assigned to Pender's Division. It halted near Berryville on June 21 where Graham's North Carolina battery joined the command. With sixteen artillery pieces now under Major Poague's command, the Battalion proceeded north with Pender's Division.

On July 1 it was at Cashtown. While the infantry marched toward Gettysburg, the battalion was detached and ordered to remain behind. At 1100 it received orders to move to Gettysburg. It arrived on the field on July 1 but did not engage.

BATTALION EQUIPMENT

15 Caissons
187 Horses
2 Forges

Divisional Artillery
Major William Thomas Poague
9 Staff and Field Officers

Major William Thomas Poague, age 27, was a teacher and then a lawyer prior to the war. He returned from his practice in Missouri to enlist in the Rockbridge Artillery of Virginia.

Divisional Artillery - Poague's Battalion of Light Artillery

Madison Light Artillery (Mississippi)
Captain George Ward
(91 troops present for duty equipped)
4 pieces

Albemarle Artillery (Virginia)
Captain James Walter Wyatt
(94 troops present for duty equipped)
4 pieces

**Company C
10th North Carolina State Troops**
Captain Joseph Graham
(125 troops present for duty equipped)
4 pieces

Brooke's Battery (Virginia)
Captain James Vass Brooke
(58 troops present for duty equipped)
4 pieces

III CSA Corps Reserve Artillery

In the major reorganisation after Chancellorsville, McIntosh's Battalion transferred from II Corps Reserve and Pegram's Battalion, which formerly had been commanded by Walker, moved from support of A.P. Hill's old Light Division. The Reserve Artillery commander, Colonel Reuben Walker, was recognised by the army's artillerymen as thoroughly deserving his promotion. Walker had been involved in every battle since First Manassas.

The various batteries were in the thick of the fighting at Chancellorsville and horse losses had been particularly severe.

III ARMY CORPS RESERVE ARTILLERY
Colonel Reuben Lindsay Walker
4 Staff and Field Officers

During the refit after that battle, Pegram's Battalion received 56 and McIntosh's Battalion received 34 horses.

The reserve, with 35 artillery pieces, departed its camps near Fredericksburg on June 15. Notable among its guns were the pair of breech-loading

RESERVE ARTILLERY EQUIPMENT

25 Caissons
390 Horses
7 Forges
2 Battery Wagons

Whitworth Rifles in Hurt's 2nd Hardaway Artillery. Imported through the blockade they were credited with a range of 10,000 yards at 30 degrees elevation. The most advanced pieces on the field, their complicated breech mechanisms often required repair and were less manoeuvrable than other rifled pieces.

The Reserve's march north was largely uneventful. Colonel Walker did not assume command until the morning of July 1.

McIntosh's Battalion of Artillery
Major David Gregg McIntosh

Hardaway Artillery (Alabama)
Captain William B. Hurt
(71 troops present for duty equipped)
2 3-inch rifled guns
2 Whitworth guns

Danville Artillery (Virginia)
Captain Robert Sidney Rice
(114 troops present for duty equipped)
4 12-pounder Napoleon Guns

2nd Rockbridge Artillery (Virginia)
Lieutenant Samuel Wallace
(67 troops present for duty equipped)
2 3-inch rifled guns
2 12-pounder Napoleon guns

Jackson's Flying Artillery (Virginia)
Captain Marmaduke Johnson
(96 troops present for duty equipped)
4 3-inch rifled guns

Pegram's Battalion of Artillery
Major William Johnson Pegram
Captain Ervin B. Brunson

PeeDee Artillery (South Carolina)
Lieutenant William E. Zimmerman
(65 troops present for duty equipped)
4 3-inch rifled guns

Crenshaw Battery (Virginia)
Captain Thomas R. Ellett
(76 troops present for duty equipped)
2 12-pounder Napoleon guns
2 12-pounder howitzers

Fredericksburg Artillery (Virginia)
Captain Edward Avenmore Marye
(71 troops present for duty equipped)
2 3-inch rifled guns
2 12-pounder Napoleon guns

Letcher Artillery (Virginia)
Captain Thomas Alexander Brander
(65 troops present for duty equipped)
2 10-pounder Parrott rifled guns
2 12-pounder Napoleon guns

Purcell Artillery (Virginia)
Captain Joseph McGraw
(89 troops present for duty equipped)
4 12-pounder Napoleon guns

III CORPS BATTLES
July 1 0800 - 1130 hrs

Disaster in the Morning

The soldiers of Heth's Division began their march to Gettysburg around 0500 hours. No-one expected to encounter serious opposition. So confident were the Confederates that five batteries belonging to Pegram's Battalion of the Artillery Reserve led the way. After the war Heth remarked that he anticipated finding only militia and that he knew "they would run as soon as we appeared." Archer's Tennessee Brigade followed the artillery and then came Davis' Brigade.

The troops marched past Pettigrew's men who had probed Gettysburg the previous day. Pettigrew's officers confirmed that ahead lay only militia. At 0730 hours the leading troops reached the bridge over Marsh Creek. Here vigilant Federal cavalry vedettes opened fire.

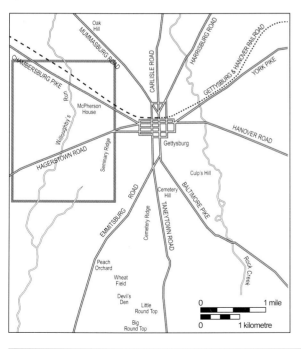

The 5th Alabama Battalion dashed across the bridge and deployed in skirmish order. Some sixty skirmishers from the 13th Alabama joined them. A 3- inch rifle belonging to the Fredericksburg Battery unlimbered on a nearby hill and began firing.

At 0800 hours, Heth's skirmish line advanced followed by Archer and Davis in road column. Buford's cavalry delayed their advance enough so that the main column did not reach Herr Ridge until 0850 hours. Here the two Brigades deployed in line of battle. Pegram's seventeen guns took station on convenient rises and began to shell McPherson's Ridge. Unknown to the rebels, eight U.S. cavalry regiments and one battery defended that ridge. The odds were roughly three to two in favour of the Confederates.

After a thirty-minute preparatory bombardment, at 0930 hours the Confederate infantry descended Herr Ridge toward Willoughby Run. Buford reported, "The two lines soon became hotly engaged." A captain in the 1st Tennessee confirmed, "we met stubborn resistance." Buford's dismounted troopers managed to slow Heth's advance until Federal infantry arrived on McPherson's Ridge.

Pegram's batteries shifted from a sporadic shelling of the woods to target the infantry of Cutler's Brigade. Meanwhile, with its right flank resting on the Chambersburg Pike, Davis' infantry steadily climbed McPherson's Ridge. Initially the Brigade line stretched from the Chambersburg Pike north for about 400 yards to Willoughby Run. From left to right the order was 55th North Carolina, 2nd Mississippi, and 42nd Mississippi. The 11th Mississippi had remained behind in Cashtown to guard the divisional trains.

The Brigade drifted to its left and it advanced. About 1020 hours the 55th North Carolina received a volley at 200 yards range from a Pennsylvania regiment. It was the first exchange of musketry between the two

0800 hrs	0900	1000	1100	1200	1300	1400	1500	1600	1700	1800
						45-47		48-49 & 50-52	53-55	

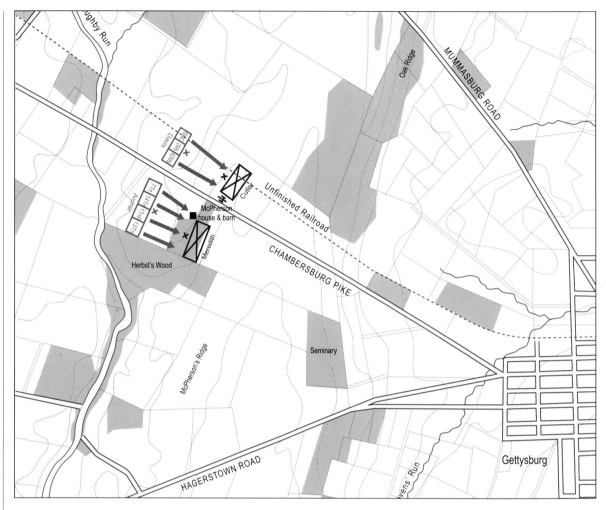

0930 hours - Davis' Brigade begins its advance along the Chambersburg Pike toward Gettysburg. To the south, Archer moves his Brigade forward toward Herbst's Wood - the exact order of deployment of his regiments is uncertain but is probably as indicated - and here encounters the Iron Brigade.

armies' infantry. Indicative of what was to come, two men of the 55th's colour guard were hit. A Mississippian related that the enemy "were in the wheat...lying down, though plainly seen." The fire-fight quickly spread until all three of Davis' regiments were engaged.

Within minutes of the beginning of this encounter, a fight between Archer's Brigade and the Union "Iron" Brigade started south of the Chambersburg Pike. The

first contact occurred in Herbst's Woods where the 1st Tennessee collided with the 2nd Wisconsin. The two regiments exchanged volleys at 50 yards range. Until this point, Archer's men believed that they merely had to brush aside a few skirmishers in order to capture the heights. As the rest of the Brigade splashed across Willoughby Run on the right of the 1st Tennessee, the appearance of more units of the Iron Brigade disabused them. Spotting the distinctive hats worn by the Iron Brigade, soldiers shouted, "There comes them old black hats! It's the Army of the Potomac, sure!"

The sudden appearance of the Iron Brigade shocked Archer's men. Heavy Federal volleys delivered at close range rapidly spread confusion among their ranks. A private in the 13th Alabama ruefully recalled, "We discovered that we had tackled a hard proposition." In its attempt to deal with the unexpected pressure, the

0800 hrs	0900	1000	1100	1200	1300	1400	1500	1600	1700	1800
							45-47	48-49 & 50-52	53-55	

Brigade became separated into two wings. Quite simply, Archer had lost control of his men.

A break occurred on the right when advancing Federals enveloped that flank. The Brigade's line unravelled until the regiments fighting on the opposite flank received the order to fall back to Willoughby Run. With the Iron Brigade in hot pursuit, the Confederates retired rapidly across the Run and back up the slope of Herr Ridge.

The Brigade lost about 75 prisoners during this phase of the fighting, not the least of whom was Brigadier-General Archer himself. Archer had been sick with a fever and was sluggish in mind and body on July 1. He had been in the midst of trying to rally his troops when captured. A Tennessee officer described him at this point as "very much exhausted with fatigue." Archer was the first of Lee's generals to experience this fate. By 1100 hours the Brigade's fight was over. Although it had not suffered too severely, it would report 160 killed and wounded for its fight on July 1 and July 3; for the balance of the day, it was of little service.

While Archer's debacle was underway, Davis' three regiments continued their struggle north of the Chambersburg Pike. The Mississippians steadily advanced into a fierce musketry. By virtue of the Brigade's northward drift during its approach march, the 55th North Carolina, on the Brigade's left flank, overlapped the opposing Union regiment. Colonel John Connally ordered his men to fix bayonets and charge.

Because some of the North Carolinians had been hidden by a fold in the ground, their charge surprised the defenders. When part of the Regiment began pouring enfilade fire against the exposed Federal left flank, the New Yorkers wavered. About 100 yards from the enemy, the 55th's standard bearer fell. Colonel Connally seized the Regiment's colours and to encourage his men further, ran ahead of them. Such a prominent target could not survive. Connally fell with two wounds. Major Alfred Belo ran up to him to provide assistance. When Belo asked if Connally was in pain, the colonel replied in the affirmative. But glancing over at the adjacent unit, the 2nd Mississippi, Connally instructed Belo to ignore him and "take the colors and keep ahead of the Mississippians."

Firing as they charged, the 55th North Carolina enveloped the Federal flank. Meanwhile, the 2nd Mississippi launched an impetuous frontal assault. A furious struggle took place around the colours of the 56th Pennsylvania. It ended with the Mississippians in possession of the flag and about 300 Union soldiers.

The three Federal regiments north of the Chambersburg Pike received orders to retire to the slopes of Oak Ridge. However, at first, the regiment nearest the railroad cut, the 147th New York, failed to receive the order. From the western edge of a wheat field about sixty yards away, the 42nd Mississippi opened fire against the isolated Federal unit. A Union survivor recalled that, "Men dropped dead, then the wounded men went to the rear before they had emptied their muskets." The 147th stood its ground until the 2nd Mississippi bore in against its uncovered right flank.

The linchpin of the Union defence at this point was the 2nd Maine Battery, which was posted on commanding terrain between the pike and the railroad cut. But the Battery stood on exposed ground. Pegram's artillery began effective counter-battery fire. The Letcher Artillery displaced 500 yards forward to provide close-range support for Davis' infantry. Around 1100 hours men of the 42nd Mississippi formed in the railroad cut and then charged to within 50 yards of the Maine Battery. Blasts of double-shotted canister repelled the attack.

Men from the 42nd dispersed into skirmish order and began to pick off gunners and horses. The battery had no answer and retired a short distance. Some of Davis' soldiers ambushed one retreating section, felling all four horses hauling one limber. The Federal artillerymen abandoned it. The rebels formed a fire-tinged gauntlet that drove the surviving gunners and their pieces from this part of the field.

At about the same time, to the north of the pike, the 147th New York yielded its position. It had faced several companies so they could oppose the Confederate flank attack. Eventually, weight of numbers stove in its flank. The cry went up, "They are flanking us again". Some of the men tried to escape via the railroad cut. A Federal private describes what ensued: they were "going along as fast as we could, but not very, for the road was so crowded...Soon the Rebels came up each side of the bank in large numbers, and we had to throw down our arms and surrender."

At this juncture, portions of the 42nd Mississippi were in the railroad cut while the balance of the Brigade was in the open to the north. Having completed their wheel to envelope the Federal flank, they faced roughly southward. The railroad cut lay directly before them.

Unknown to Davis' men, three yankee regiments had responded to their success by moving from their posi-

0800 hrs	0900	1000	1100	1200	1300	1400	1500	1600	1700	1800
							45-47	48-49 & 50-52	53-55	

tion along McPherson's Ridge to face north toward the railroad cut. Spearheaded by the Iron Brigade's 6th Wisconsin, these regiments counter-attacked toward the cut.

The 6th Wisconsin's fire caused the Confederate line to sway and bend. Recovering, the survivors made for the natural protection of the railroad cut. The sudden reversal of fortune disordered Davis' Brigade. Part of the difficulty was due to leadership. Both the colonels and lieutenant-colonels of the 2nd Mississippi and 55th North Carolina were casualties. Seven of nine field officers were also casualties by 1200 hours.

Worse, inexperienced brigade commander Joe Davis had lost control of his men during their abortive pursuit. Consequently, men of the 2nd and 42nd Mississippi poured into the presumed shelter of the railroad cut where they stood, recalled Major John Blair who commanded the 2nd Mississippi at this point, "jumbled together without regard to regiment or company."

With the Federal counter-attack approaching the cut, Davis ordered a retreat. The lack of officers plus the chaos of battle caused the order to be imperfectly understood. Some men retired while others remained in the cut. In places the cut was so deep that the rebels could fire only with great difficulty. Yet enough were able to wield their muskets effectively so that in the course of a 175 pace advance, the 6th Wisconsin lost 180 men.

A small group of Wisconsin soldiers occupied the cut's eastern side and opened a telling enfilade fire. New Yorkers overran the western end. A Federal colonel approached the cut at a point where it was about four feet deep and looked down to see "hundreds of rebels." Union soldiers shouted out to the trapped men of the 2nd and 42nd Mississippi, "Throw down your muskets! Down with your muskets!"

As the rebels began to surrender, a desperate struggle was taking place for the colours of the 2nd Mississippi. The Confederate colour bearer relates, "My color guards were all killed or wounded in less than five minutes, and also my colors were shot more than a dozen times, and the flag staff was hit and splintered two or three times. Just about that time a squad of soldiers made a rush for my colors and our men did their duty. They were all killed or wounded, but they still rushed for the colors with one of the most deadly struggles that was ever witnessed during any battle in the war. They still kept rushing for my flag and there were over a dozen shot down like sheep, in their madly rush

The outbreak of war prevented the completion of the Gettysburg and Hanover Railroad's line west of Gettysburg. It was a mixture of grades and cuts, designed to smooth the route. During the battle the cuts would become first a false safe-haven and later an obstruction to the Confederate forces .

for the colors...Over a dozen men fell killed or wounded, and then a large man made a rush for me and the flag. As I tore the flag from the staff he took hold of me and the color. The firing was still going on and kept up for several minutes after the flag was taken from me."

About 600 Confederates in the railroad cut were captured. The remainder of the Brigade retired in considerable disorder to Herr Ridge. Overall, the Brigade was so shaken, that Heth judged it inadvisable to place it in the battle line for the rest of July 1.

Referring to the spirit of the army in July 1863, Major-General Heth recalled, "There was not an officer or soldier in the Army of Northern Virginia, from General Lee to the drummer boy, who did not believe...that it was able to drive the Federal army into the Atlantic Ocean."

The combats during the morning of July 1 chastened Heth and the brigadiers involved. In his after-action report, Heth referred to the debacle of Archer's and Davis' Brigades with the words, "The enemy had now been felt, and found to be in heavy force in and around Gettysburg."

Heth still had two uncommitted brigades. But, under orders not to bring on a general engagement, he remained on the defensive. McIntosh's Battalion arrived and deployed alongside Pegram's batteries and both batteries kept up a desultory fire for the remainder of the morning.

0800 hrs	0900	1000	1100	1200	1300	1400	1500	1600	1700	1800
						45-47	48-49 & 50-52		53-55	

III CORPS BATTLES
July 1 1430 - 1600 hrs

Afternoon Breakthrough - Heth Tries Again

Lee arrived on the field shortly after 1300 hours and confirmed Heth's decision to remain in position and wait. Then the Confederates on Herr Ridge saw the yankees begin to shift to face a new threat from the northeast. This was caused by Rodes' Division arriving on the field. When that Division met considerable opposition, Heth found Lee and asked, "Rodes is very heavily engaged, had I not better attack?" With his army still not concentrated, Lee was still unready to bring on a general engagement. Only after Early's opportune arrival changed the battle's calculus, did Lee permit first Heth, and then Pender, to advance.

Until that time, Heth's Division remained north of the Chambersburg Pike with the duty of intercepting stragglers and returning them to the battle line. Later, when Daniel's Brigade charged past and some of the soldiers called out for Davis' men to join, the demoralised soldiers declined.

For his second assault against McPherson's Ridge, Heth expected little from Davis' shattered brigade. He stationed Brockenbrough's Brigade on the Division's left, with its own left flank anchored on the Chambersburg Pike. Pettigrew's large Brigade manned the centre. Archer's Brigade supported Pettigrew's right. At about 1430 hours these units descended from Herr Ridge and charged toward McPherson's Ridge.

From the west of Willoughby Run, nine batteries belonging to the Confederate Army's Reserve Artillery supported the advance. Pegram's guns occupied a low crest just south of the Chambersburg Pike. The Danville Artillery and the Whitworth section of the Hardaway Artillery joined these five batteries at this position. The Jackson Flying Artillery and the 3-inch rifled section of the Hardaway Artillery took station on a commanding rise closer to the Fairfield Road. The

2nd Rockbridge Artillery deployed just north of the Chambersburg Pike. At first these guns opened a slow and methodical fire. When the Federal artillery uncovered, their fire intensified. At one point one of Garnett's batteries replaced a reserve battery because it had consumed all of its ammunition. Overall, the Confederate artillery provided excellent service along this front. However, the lack of firing positions kept Lane's, Poague's, Cutt's, and all except the one battery of Garnett's, from joining in. They all remained in reserve well back on the Chambersburg Pike.

When the infantry went forward, Brockenbrough's advance apparently lacked conviction. His Virginians initially headed toward Stone's Brigade. After a stern but brief contest with Stone's skirmishers, the brigade neared the crest of McPherson's Ridge. A small quar-

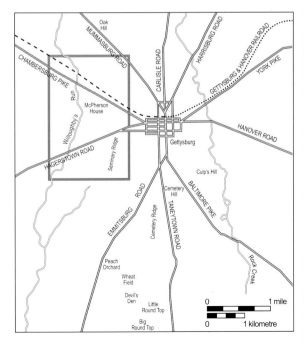

0800 hrs	0900	1000	1100	1200	1300	1400	1500	1600	1700	1800
						45-47	48-49 & 50-52	53-55		

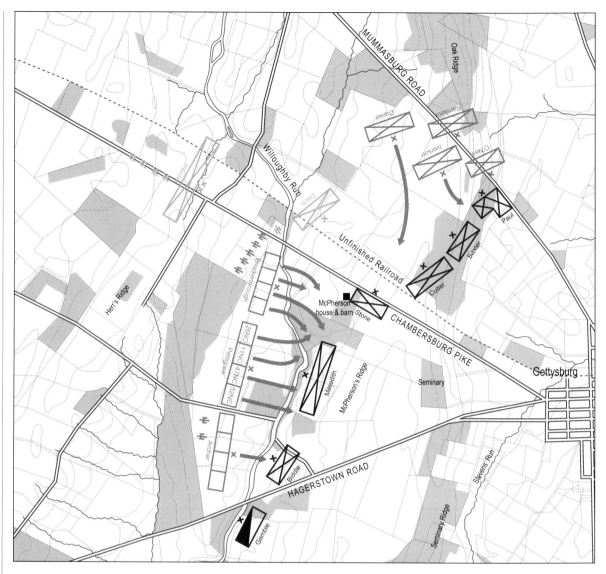

Approx. 1430 hours - Heth launches three of his brigades in a second attempt to wrest McPherson's Ridge from the Federals.

ry compelled it to oblique to the south where it entered Herbst's Woods. Here the Virginians were content to take shelter and engage in a musketry duel against Stone's men and elements of the Iron Brigade.

The Brigade was successful in fixing the defenders to its front. The 150th Pennsylvania, which had been facing in the direction of the railroad cut, shifted to meet the threat posed by Brockenbrough's Brigade. This left a gap that Daniel's Brigade of Rodes' Division would

exploit. Only after Daniel's men and Pettigrew's Brigade drove back the yankees did Brockenbrough's Brigade advance again. During a limited pursuit its men captured two enemy colours. For the day the Brigade lost only about 100 men.

In contrast, Pettigrew's Brigade entered the fight with zeal. They were following the route taken earlier by Archer's Brigade. Like that unit, Pettigrew's men confronted soldiers of the Iron Brigade in Herbst's Woods. In addition, they faced Biddle's Brigade en echelon to the left rear of the Iron Brigade.

Initially, the veteran North Carolinians exploited the dangling flank presented by the 19th Indiana, the left-

0800 hrs	0900	1000	1100	1200	1300	1400	1500	1600	1700	1800
						45-47	48-49 & 50-52	53-55		

most unit of the Iron Brigade. When they drove that Regiment back, it uncovered the flank of the adjacent Federal unit. That regiment, the 24th Michigan, changed front to the left while under a murderous fire. The rebel line was so close that the yankees could hear its colonel, probably Colonel Marshall of the 52nd, calling out, "Give 'em hell boys!" When a bullet knocked this officer's hat off, he calmly caught it before it touched the ground and resumed his strident shouts.

Meanwhile, the balance of Pettigrew's Brigade fought in the fields south of Herbst's Woods and amidst the trees themselves. For the next 60 minutes a terrible struggle took place, often at ranges as short as 20 paces. Here the 26th North Carolina lost more than half its strength including the death of Colonel Burgwyn and a serious wound to Lieutenant-Colonel Lane. Eleven men carrying the 26th's colours were shot down. In Company F, 88 out of 89 men were hit by hostile fire while the remaining soldier was knocked unconscious by concussion from an exploding shell. Among three sets of twins who served in the regiment, five died.

The 11th North Carolina had a similar fate. One com-

The Confederate attack on the stone barn at McPherson's Farm.

pany lost two of three officers and thirty-one of thirty five men. Amidst such losses, the advance of the 11th and 26th stalled. However, they had inflicted enormous casualties upon their foes. The regiment opposing the 26th lost 79% of its strength.

While this slaughter took place, Archer's Brigade made a tentative advance on the Division's right. When the Federal cavalry worked around the Brigade's right flank, Colonel Fry who now commanded the Brigade, changed front to face this threat. This effectively removed the Brigade from active participation in the fight for McPherson's Ridge.

Eventually, Pettigrew's 52nd North Carolina worked its way around the defenders left flank while the 47th North Carolina provided frontal pressure. Having battled through what they perceived to be three successive defensive positions, Pettigrew's Brigade gained the crest of McPherson's Ridge. By the time the yankees ceded the ridge, Heth's Division as a whole had suffered close to 40% losses.

0800 hrs	0900	1000	1100	1200	1300	1400	1500	1600	1700	1800
						45-47	48-49 & 50-52		53-55	

III CORPS BATTLES
July 1 1600 - 1630 hrs

Afternoon Breakthrough - Pender Goes In

Heth's Division fought the battle for McPherson's Ridge unaided by Pender's Division. By the time the Union defence began breaking up, it was close to 1600 hours. Around that time, corps commander A.P. Hill ordered Pender's Division to pass through Heth's depleted ranks and continue the advance. This took time. Not until about 1600 hours did the Division move past Pettigrew's Brigade, Heth's most advanced troops, and begin its assault on the new Union position on Seminary Ridge.

The Confederate artillery had been actively supporting Heth's attack. At one point, two batteries belonging to McIntosh's Battalion moved forward to a hollow just east of Willoughby Run in order to enfilade the Federal defenders of the railroad cut. Other batteries belonging to both McIntosh's and Pegram's Battalions

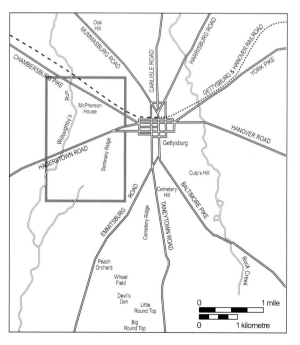

crossed their fire with III Corps guns of Carter's Battalion to help Rodes clear Oak Ridge.

Although the well-sited artillery provided fine close-support, it was up to the infantry to drive the defenders from Seminary Ridge. Pender's Division formed a line that stretched for about one mile from the Chambersburg Pike to the Fairfield Road. From left to right the order was Scales, Perrin, Lane, with Thomas held in reserve to exploit any successes. A Federal artilleryman describes the sight of Scales and Perrin advances against the ridge: "the enemy filed in two strong columns out of the woods, about 500 yards to our front, and marched steadily down to our left until they outflanked us nearly a third of a mile. They then formed in double line of battle, and came directly up the crest."

Scales' North Carolinians had to fight through the retreating remnants of the Iron Brigade. Although this did not prove easy, the fact that the North Carolinians were advancing close on the heels of the retreating enemy troops initially sheltered them from some of the Union artillery fire. However, once the front cleared of retreating enemy infantry, Scales' Brigade met a terrible fate.

They advanced straight at the massed artillery of Union I Corps near the Seminary. Directly in front of the Brigade were 12 guns that were packed so tightly that hardly five yards separated the pieces. Additional batteries extended the artillery line to Scales' right. Another section of Federal artillery delivered enfilade fire against the Brigade's left flank.

Scales' men marched through a barrage of case shot and shell thickened by musketry volleys. At the double quick, the Brigade advanced into canister range. When they were within 75 to 100 yards of the yankee guns, the Union artillery opened a devastating fire.

Scales relates, "Here the brigade encountered a most terrific fire of grape and shell on our flank, and grape

0800 hrs	0900	1000	1100	1200	1300	1400	1500	1600	1700	1800
							45-47	48-49 & 50-52	53-55	

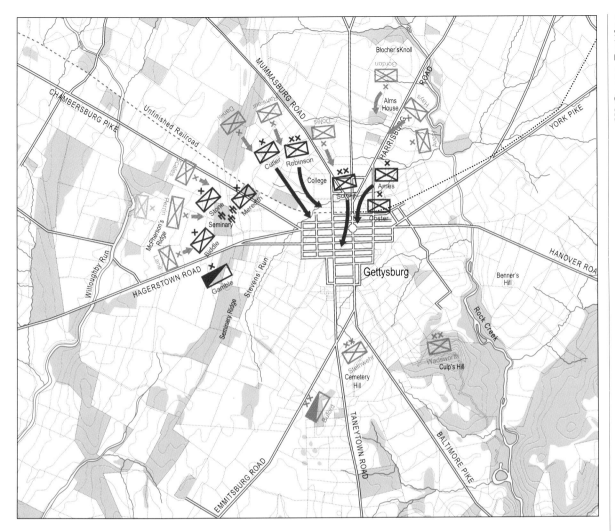

and musketry in our front. Every discharge made sad havoc in our line."

When a shell tore off the right arm of the 13th North Carolina's colour-bearer, he shifted his standard to his other arm and continued while screaming, "Forward, forward!" Scales himself was wounded in the leg. In a span of about fifteen minutes, Scales' Brigade suffered more than 500 casualties including 55 of 56 field officers. The solid lines dissolved into squad-sized knots.

Only with difficulty could the survivors be rallied through the exertions of General Pender and his staff as well as the wounded General Scales. Later in the evening, the acting brigade commander could find only 500 men, and they in a "depressed, dilapidated, and almost unorganised condition."

On the opposite flank, Lane's Brigade overlapped the

Approx. 1600 hours - Pender commits his Division against Seminary Ridge as the Federal's northern front crumbles.

opposing infantry. However, Gamble's Union cavalry, which was posted at right angles to Lane's line of advance, remained very active. As the Brigade advanced it drifted to its right and away from the main combat along Seminary Ridge. Emerging from the woods, the Brigade received enfilading fire that considerably slowed its advance. The Brigade then double-quicked ahead and drove off the cavalry occupying the woods to its front.

Lane's Brigade had manoeuvred very cautiously. At one point the rarest of events on a Civil War battlefield occurred when some of Lane's men apparently formed

0800 hrs	0900	1000	1100	1200	1300	1400	1500	1600	1700	1800
							45-47	48-49 & 50-52	53-55	

The Cemetary Gate House. It is ironic that close by stood a sign that read "All persons found using firearms in these grounds will be prosecuted with the utmost vigor of the law."

square in anticipation of receiving a cavalry charge! The Brigade's fitful advance contributed little to the Confederate victory on July 1, a day during which it lost about 120 men.

The heroes of the hour were the soldiers of Perrin's Brigade. They had to cross about 600 yards of clear ground to reach the defenders atop Seminary Ridge. Perrin instructed his regimental commanders not to allow the men to fire until they were ordered.

The Brigade aligned on Scales' adjacent Brigade and advanced about 400 yards through sporadic artillery fire. After crossing a swale about 200 yards in front of the Seminary, some of the yankee artillery that had been decimating Scales' men turned to fire at Perrin's troops from their left front. Directly ahead stood Biddle's Brigade, who manned some hastily prepared earthworks. They opened fire as well.

A divisional staff officer describes what took place: "Upon ascending a hill in front, the brigade was met by a furious storm of musketry and shell from infantry posed behind temporary breastworks and artillery from batteries to the left...The brigade steadily advanced at a charge, reserving its fire as ordered...The brigade, in crossing a line of fencing, received a most withering and destructive fire, but continued to charge without returning the fire of the enemy until reaching the edge of the grove which crowns the crest of the ridge."

Perrin's order to charge without pausing to return fire allowed the Brigade to advance rapidly through the beaten zone. But it had been costly. While crossing the fence, the Brigade received what Perrin later described as "the most destructive fire I have ever been exposed to." In its first try, Perrin's Brigade could not overcome the Union line. The only man to reach the earthworks was a standard bearer. The defenders had fired so fast that their musket barrels were heated red hot.

With his Brigade driven back by enemy fire, Perrin regrouped his men. Since Scales' men had been repulsed, he saw he would not receive any support on his left. Lane's inability to push aside the Federal cavalry meant that the Brigade also would not receive support on its right. However, Perrin observed that his line overlapped the left flank of the infantry opposing him. In addition, he noticed a gap where Biddle's Brigade did not link up with the Federal cavalry on the Union left. He also understood his men's capabilities. As one unit historian later wrote, "There was no giving back on our part."

Perrin shifted his units to exploit this gap by dividing his Brigade into two wings. While one wing again attacked straight ahead, the other, personally led by Perrin, advanced toward the gap. Here the 1st South Carolina breached the Federal defences. Its success caused the Federal line to begin to collapse.

Perrin had his finger on the battle's pulse. He ordered the 12th and 13th South Carolina to attack obliquely to his right to charge some cavalry defending a stone wall on Biddle's left. "They rushed up the crest of the hill and the stone fence, driving everything before them". Then the 1st and 14th wheeled to their left to pour an enfilade fire into the Union line at the Seminary. Their fire drove off the Union artillery and its infantry supports. Perrin's success caused the Federal commander to order a retreat from Seminary Ridge at about 1630 hours. After a pursuit to the outskirts of Gettysburg, Perrin halted his Brigade to reorganise it. The South Carolinians were spent and would not participate in any further combat on July 1.

Perrin's Brigade suffered almost all of its 577 losses on July 1, about 30% of its strength. Every one of the colour-sergeants taken into battle died at the front of his regiment. In the Division's after action report, a staff major wrote, "Too much credit cannot be awarded to Colonel Perrin and the splendid brigade under his command for the manner and spirit with which this attack was conducted."

0800 hrs	0900	1000	1100	1200	1300	1400	1500	1600	1700	1800
							45-47	48-49 & 50-52	53-55	

Stuart's Cavalry Division

The origins of Stuart's Cavalry Division dated back to October 1861, when newly promoted Brigadier-General Stuart took command of the army's cavalry brigade. Among the forces under his command were two Virginia regiments commanded by officers who were to lead brigades themselves; Colonel Fitzhugh Lee and Colonel W.H.F. Lee. Stuart

Major-General James Ewell Brown Stuart, an aggressive and flamboyant 30-year-old, played the part of a chivalrous cavalier to good effect both in battle and in the public eye. The Virginian was a brilliant light cavalry commander.

led select units on a ride around McClellan's army, an exploit that made the young cavalier's reputation. The Brigade's success during the Seven Days' Battles, and Stuart's obvious capacity as a cavalry commander prompted Robert E. Lee to expand Stuart's command to a division of two brigades under Brigadier-General

CAVALRY CORPS
Major-General James Ewell Brown Stuart
20 Staff and Field Officers

Hampton's Brigade 1,751
Brigadier-General Wade Hampton/
Colonel Laurence Simmons Baker

Robertson's Brigade 966
Brigadier-General
Beverly Holcombe Robertson

Jones' Brigade 1,713
Brigadier-General William Edmondson Jones

Fitzhugh Lee's Brigade 1,913
Brigadier-General Fitzhugh Lee

Jenkins' Brigade 1,179
Brigadier-General Albert Gallatin Jenkins/
Colonel Milton J. Ferguson

W.H.F. Lee's Brigade 1,173
Colonel John Randolph Chambliss, Jr.

Beckham's Battalion of Artillery 434
Major Robert Franklin Beckham

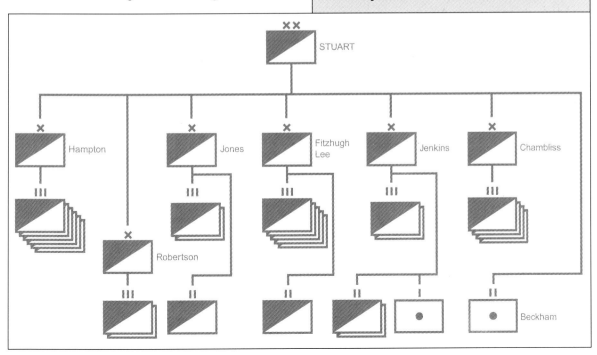

HAMPTON'S BRIGADE
Brigadier-General Wade Hampton/
Colonel Laurence Simmons Baker
5 Staff and Field Officers

9th North Carolina State Troops (1st Cavalry)
Colonel Laurence Simmons Baker/
Lieutenant-Colonel James B. Gordon
407 troops present for duty equipped

1st South Carolina Regiment of Cavalry
Colonel John Logan Black
339 troops present for duty equipped

2nd South Carolina Regiment of Cavalry
Colonel Mathew Calbraith Butler
186 troops present for duty equipped

Cobb's (Georgia) Legion
Colonel Pierce B.M. Young
330 troops present for duty equipped

Jefferson Davis Legion (Mississippi)
Colonel Joseph Frederick Waring
246 troops present for duty equipped

Phillip's (Georgia) Legion
Lieutenant-Colonel William W. Rich
238 troops present for duty equipped

ROBERTSON'S BRIGADE
(not engaged at Gettysburg)
Brigadier-General Beverly Holcombe Robertson
4 Staff and Field Officers

59th Regiment North Carolina Troops (4th Cavalry)
Colonel Dennis Dozier Ferebee
504 troops present for duty equipped

63rd Regiment North Carolina Troops (5th Cavalry)
Colonel Peter G. Evans
458 troops present for duty equipped

his supply base at Catlett's Station. Always eager for public acclaim, Stuart led the Division, now expanded by the addition of Brigadier-General Beverly Robertson's Brigade, on a second ride around McClellan during the Maryland Campaign of 1862.

For the Fredericksburg Campaign, Brigadier-General W.H.F. Lee's Brigade joined the Division. After this campaign, elements of the Division raided to within a few miles of the defences of Washington, D.C.

Army commander Lee summoned three Virginia cavalry brigades to strengthen his mounted arm for the invasion of the North. They included Brigadier-General Albert Jenkins' Brigade, which previously had operated in the mountains of western Virginia. Its troopers were accustomed to guerrilla warfare featuring raid and counter-raid. Assigned to screen the advance of Ewell's Corps, Jenkins' Brigade failed dismally, its men preferring to pillage civilians rather than to serve as a useful advance guard. In contrast, Brigadier-General

Wade Hampton and Brigadier-General Fitzhugh Lee. Stuart himself received a promotion to major-general.

During the Second Manassas Campaign, the Division manoeuvred around Pope's northern flank to strike at

JONES' BRIGADE
(not engaged at Gettysburg)
Brigadier-General William Edmondson Jones
4 Staff and Field Officers

6th Regiment Virginia Cavalry
Major Cabell Edward Flournoy
625 troops present for duty equipped

7th Regiment Virginia Cavalry
Colonel Thomas A. Marshall, Jr.
428 troops present for duty equipped

11th Regiment Virginia Cavalry
Colonel Lunsford Lindsay Lomax
424 troops present for duty equipped

FITZHUGH LEE'S BRIGADE
Brigadier-General Fitzhugh Lee
4 Staff and Field Officers

1st Maryland Cavalry Battalion
Major Harry Gilmor
310 troops present for duty equipped

3rd Regiment Virginia Cavalry
Colonel Thomas Howerton Owen
210 troops present for duty equipped

1st Regiment Virginia Cavalry
Colonel James Henry Drake
310 troops present for duty equipped

4th Regiment Virginia Cavalry
Colonel Williams Carter Wickham
544 troops present for duty equipped

2nd Regiment Virginia Cavalry
Colonel Thomas Taylor Munford
385 troops present for duty equipped

5th Regiment Virginia Cavalry
Colonel Thomas Lafayette Rosser
150 troops present for duty equipped

William Jones' Brigade had previously been associated with the Division but generally had served on detached duty.

An engagement that was to prove critical to the Gettysburg Campaign occurred at Brandy Station on June 9, 1863. A Federal cavalry offensive surprised Stuart's command and the biggest cavalry engagement of the war ensued. Here, along with about 530 other casualties, Robert E. Lee's son, "Rooney" Lee, received a serious wound. Colonel John Chambliss, who formerly had led the 13th Virginia Cavalry, assumed command. Although Brandy Station was a tactical draw, the fact that Stuart had been surprised both embarrassed him and brought down a barrage of popular criticism. He resolved to lead his Division on some dashing exploit to remove the stain.

First the Division fought a series of combats along the Blue Ridge Mountain passes in an effort to screen the infantry's march through the Shenandoah Valley. With the Federal cavalry blocked from penetrating west of the Blue Ridge, Stuart proposed to Lee that he could operate east of the mountains to harass Hooker's army as it marched to parallel Lee's advance.

On June 22 Lee wrote to Stuart. If Stuart determined that Hooker was moving northward he could, leaving two brigades to guard the mountain passes, "move with the other three into Maryland, and take position on General Ewell's right, place yourself in communication with him, guard his flank, and keep him informed of the enemy's movements." The next day Lee added, "You will, however, be able to judge whether you can pass around their army without hindrance, doing them all the damage you can." Stuart seized upon this as permitting a grand raid that would restore his reputation.

Stuart chose his three favourite brigades; Hampton's, Fitz Lee's, and "Rooney" Lee's (commanded by

JENKINS' BRIGADE
Brigadier-General Albert Gallatin Jenkins
4 Staff and Field Officers

14th Regiment Virginia Cavalry
Colonel Charles Edmonson Thorburn
265 troops present for duty equipped

34th Battalion Virginia Cavalry
Lieutenant-Colonel Vincent Addison Witcher
172 troops present for duty equipped

16th Regiment Virginia Cavalry
Colonel Milton J. Ferguson
265 troops present for duty equipped

36th Battalion Virginia Cavalry
Colonel Charles E. Thorburn
125 troops present for duty equipped

17th Regiment Virginia Cavalry
Colonel William Henderson French
241 troops present for duty equipped

Kanawha Horse Artillery (Virginia)
Captain Thomas E. Jackson
107 troops present for duty equipped

WILLIAM HENRY FITZHUGH LEE'S BRIGADE
Colonel John Randolph Chambliss, Jr.
4 Staff and Field Officers

19th North Carolina State Troops (2nd Cavalry)
Lieutenant-Colonel William H.F. Payne
145 troops present for duty equipped

10th Regiment Virginia Cavalry
Colonel James Lucius Davis
236 troops present for duty equipped

9th Regiment Virginia Cavalry
Colonel Richard Lee Turberville Beale
490 troops present for duty equipped

13th Regiment Virginia Cavalry
Lieutenant-Colonel Jefferson Curle Phillips
298 troops present for duty equipped

Chambliss) for a ride around the Union army. Since William Jones was a skilled outpost commander, Stuart detailed his brigade to guard the passes along with the less experienced brigade commanded by Beverly Robertson. The problem was that the indolent Robertson was Jones' senior. This may have contributed to a communications breakdown when these brigadiers failed to relay Stuart's intelligence regarding Hooker's move north.

The three chosen brigades departed Salem, Virginia on June 25. The column skirted the Washington defences but was further delayed by the need to march between large formations of hostile infantry. On June 28 it crossed the Potomac River. The Federal army now lay between Stuart and Lee. At Rockville, Maryland, the cavalry intercepted a Federal supply train and captured 125 wagons. The wagons' presence slowed the cavalry's march.

On the morning of June 29, after a night march of some 20 miles, the van of the column entered Hood's Mill. Here they wasted more time tearing up railroad tracks and burning bridges. Uncertain of Ewell's location, the column marched north 15 miles to Westminster on the main road from Baltimore to Gettysburg. Here a brisk combat occurred with a Federal cavalry detachment. The cavalry moved toward Hanover on June 30 where another combat took place. To avoid more enemy cavalry, the column had to detour east and then north. Stuart ordered the Division to perform another tiring night march to try to rejoin Lee.

On June 28, Robert E. Lee still did not know that the Federal army had been on the move north of the Potomac since June 26, because the officer who habitually had kept him apprised of enemy movements was out of touch. To virtually every officer who came to headquarters Lee asked, 'Can you tell me where General Stuart is?'

Divisional Artillery - Beckham's Battalion of Artillery
Major Robert Franklin Beckham
9 Staff and Field Officers

1st Stuart Horse Artillery (Virginia)
Captain James Breathed
(106 troops present for duty equipped)
4 pieces

Washington Artillery (South Carolina)
Captain James Franklin Hart
(107 troops present for duty equipped)
3 pieces

Ashby Artillery (Virginia)
Captain Roger Preston Chew
(99 troops - not engaged at Gettysburg)
4 pieces

2nd Stuart Horse Artillery (Virginia)
Captain William Morrell McGregor
(106 troops present for duty equipped)
4 pieces

2nd Maryland Artillery (Baltimore Light)
Captain William H. Griffin
(106 troops present for duty equipped)
4 pieces

Beauregard Rifles Stuart Horse Artillery (Virginia)
Captain Marcellus Newton Moorman
(112 troops - not engaged at Gettysburg)
4 pieces

Stuart's Cavalry Division - Imboden's Command

In preparation for the invasion of the North, three Virginia cavalry brigades joined the Army of Northern Virginia's mounted forces. Brigadier-General John Imboden's small command was one of these brigades. Previously, the Brigade had operated independently, usually in the Shenandoah Valley. Its primary missions had involved raiding and defending against Federal incursions from West Virginia. It was less well trained and disciplined than those cavalry brigades which routinely served with the army. Neither Lee nor Stuart had great confidence in the Brigade. Since it had limited experience in a pitched battle with

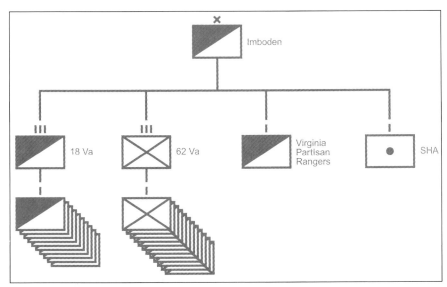

Brigadier-General John Daniel Imboden, was a 40-year-old lawyer and legislator from Virginia.

IMBODEN'S COMMAND
Brigadier-General John Daniel Imboden
4 Staff and Field Officers
2,245 troops guarding baggage -
not engaged at Gettysburg

18th Regiment Virginia Cavalry
Colonel George William Imboden
914 troops present for duty equipped

62nd Regiment
Virginia Mounted Infantry
Colonel George Hugh Smith
1,095 troops present for duty equipped

Virginia Partisan Rangers
Captain John Hanson McNeill
90 troops present for duty equipped

McClanahan's Battery
Captain John H. McClanahan
142 troops present for duty equipped

veteran foes, Lee planned to limit it to secondary assignments involving raiding, foraging, and rear-area guard duty.

During the Gettysburg Campaign, the Brigade operated west of the army's line of march. Specifically, it was to conduct raids to damage the Baltimore and Ohio Railroad and to collect livestock to nourish the army. It had some success tearing up the railroad and the Chesapeake and Ohio Canal at Cumberland, Maryland on June 16. June 24 found it marching north from Martinsburg, West Virginia toward the Potomac. Imboden had discretionary orders to join Ewell's advance into Pennsylvania. After crossing the Potomac at Cherry Run Ford, about eight miles west of Hancock, Maryland, the Brigade continued to forage while screening Lee's left flank. It showed little regard for personal property, its troopers looting freely.

On the night of June 28, the Brigade camped about 15 miles west of Chambersburg, Pennsylvania. It remained there until summoned to Chambersburg to guard the army's rear. Its tardy arrival on the evening of July 1 delayed Pickett's departure from Chambersburg to Gettysburg.

WARGAMING GETTYSBURG - DAY 1

To fight a well known battle like Gettysburg with historical miniatures on a tabletop presents a considerable challenge. Students of the battle recognize the grand tactical errors that the rival commanders committed and are unlikely to repeat them. If given free play, a Confederate player, unlike Heth, will probably put in every man to overwhelm the outnumbered Union cavalry, bypass opposition where necessary, and speed to capture the vital high ground south of Gettysburg. Tactically, few players will replicate Davis' blunder and enter the railroad cut if it is defined as a soldiers' trap, nor will they charge past a defended position, like Iverson, only to receive a killing enfilade fire. If they are playing the Federal side, it is doubtful that a gamer will perform like Howard and Barlow and move onto the plain north of Gettysburg, leaving a flank dangling so that Early can crush it.

Quite simply, unless one plays an historically naive opponent, it is very difficult to duplicate the conditions, the fog of war, that plagued the generals on July 1. Remember July 1 was an encounter battle. Neither side knew what they opposed and what was the significant terrain that would play an important role on subsequent days.

To fight the entire first day, it is probably necessary to create numerous artificial rules to force gamers to conform to the constraints and manoeuvres of the historical generals.

Consequently, the first day is most enjoyably wargamed as a series of intense tactical challenges. Buford versus Davis and Archer presents a classic delaying action. Davis and Archer against Meredith and Cutler should be a stern test of infantry tactics. On the plain north of Gettysburg, deploy the XI Corps in its historical position and see what Early supported by Doles' hard-fighting Georgians and Carter's artillery can accomplish.

The point in all of these scenarios is to compare a player's performance with that of his historical counterpart. What can the player accomplish in an equivalent amount of time and at what cost?

Turning to the tactical influences that dominated American Civil War battles, Gettysburg is notable as one of the few relatively open-field battles. Whereas the typical battle took place in wooded terrain, the cleared fields around Gettysburg presented more sweeping vistas. This explains the extraordinary impact of the Confederate artillery. They made full use of their long-range hitting power by occupying commanding elevations and delivering punishing enfilade fire.

Gaming the first day at Gettysburg offers the opportunity to play skirmish and tactical battles. Leave the challenge of corps and army command for July 2 and 3.

SELECT BIBLIOGRAPHY

Coddington, Edwin B. *The Gettysburg Campaign: A Study in Command.* New York: Charles Scribner's Sons, 1968

Hartwig, D. Scott. "Guts and Good Leadership: The Action at the Railroad Cut, July 1, 1863," *Gettysburg*", No. 1 (July 1989) 5-14.

Hassler, Warren W., Jr. *Crisis at the Crossroads: The First Day at Gettysburg.* University, AL: University of Alabama Press, 1970.

Luvas, Jay and Harold W. Nelson, eds. *The U.S. Army War College Guide to the Battle of Gettysburg.* Carlisle, PA: South Mountain Press, 1986.

Shue, Richard S. *Morning at Willoughby Run, July 1, 1863.* Gettysburg: Thomas Publications, 1995.

Smith, Carl, *Gettysburg 1863 High Tide of the Confederacy,* London: Osprey Publishing, (1998)

Tagg, Larry. *The Generals of Gettysburg.* Campbell, CA: Savas Publishing, 1998.

U.S. War Department. *War of the Rebellion: A Compilation of the Official Records of the Union and Confederate Armies. Series I, vol. 27.* Washington: Government Printing Office, 1889.

Wise, Jennings Cropper. *The Long Arm of Lee.* 2 vols. Lynchburg, VA: J.P. Bell Co., 1915.

PICTURE CREDITS